# UPRIGHT DOWNTIME

## MAKING WISE CHOICES
## ABOUT ENTERTAINMENT

BRIAN HAND

BOB JONES
UNIVERSITY PRESS

Greenville, South Carolina

## Library of Congress Cataloging-in-Publication Data

Hand, Brian R., 1975–
  Upright downtime : making wise choices about entertainment / Brian Hand.
    p. cm.
  Summary: "A study on what the Bible says about entertainment in the Christian life"—Provided by publisher.
  ISBN 978-1-59166-856-5 (perfect bound pbk. : alk. paper)
  1. Amusements—Religious aspects—Christianity. 2. Amusements Biblical teaching. 3. Christianity and culture. 4. Pleasure—Religious aspects—Christianity. I. Title.

  BV4597.H28 2008
  241'.65—dc22

                                                            2008024701

The fact that materials produced by other publishers may be referred to in this volume does not constitute an endorsement of the content or theological position of materials produced by such publishers.

All Scripture is quoted from the Authorized King James Version unless otherwise noted.

NASB: Scripture taken from the NEW AMERICAN STANDARD BIBLE®, Copyright © 1960, 1962, 1963, 1968, 1971, 1972, 1973, 1975, 1977, 1995 by The Lockman Foundation. Used by permission.

NIV: Scripture taken from the HOLY BIBLE, NEW INTERNATIONAL VERSION®. Copyright © 1973, 1978, 1984 by International Bible Society. Used by permission of Zondervan Publishing House. All rights reserved.

**Upright Downtime: Making Wise Choices About Entertainment**
Brian Hand

Design by Rita Golden
Page layout by Michael Boone

© 2008 BJU Press
Greenville, South Carolina 29614
Bob Jones University Press is a division of BJU Press

Printed in the United States of America
All rights reserved

ISBN 978-1-59166-856-5

15   14   13   12   11   10   9   8   7   6   5   4   3   2   1

*To my children,*
*Grace and Daniel,*
*who provide for me daily*
*the best entertainment*

# CONTENTS

# PREFACE

Faithful Christians in every generation hunger for *Biblical Discernment for Difficult Issues*, the title of this book series authored by the faculty of Bob Jones University Seminary. The true disciple thirsts for a life that reflects Christ's love for others while striving to maintain loyalty to God's revealed Truth, the Scriptures. But as every mature Christian soon learns, demonstrating both God's compassion and God's holiness in this life is a balance that is never easy to strike.

Our propensity to wander from the right path is enough to alarm any honest follower of Christ. How quickly in our pursuit of holiness we do race into the darkness of a harsh, unforgiving condemnation of others who somehow lack the light we enjoy. And how tragically inclined we all are to slip, while on the narrow way, from the firm ground of genuine compassion into the mire of an unbiblical naiveté or an unwise sentimentality. Only by God's grace can the believer combine that loving compassion and that pursuit of a rigorous holiness into one life to bring the true "light of the knowledge of the glory of God in the face of Jesus Christ" to a needy church and a lost world.

The aim of this series is to provide help in finding this right, discerning balance in spiritual life without sacrificing one crucial emphasis in Scripture for another. While written in an easy-to-read style, these works attempt to combine mature, penetrating theological thought with thorough research. They aim to provide both a fact-intensive exposition of Scripture and a piercing application of it to real human experience. Hopefully those who read will find themselves making significant strides forward on the way to a renewed mind and a transformed life for the glory of Christ.

Stephen J. Hankins, Dean
Bob Jones University Seminary

# 1

# A Background to Entertainment

With 97.5 million viewers, Super Bowl XLII was the most-watched American sporting event to date. This audience fell short of the record 106 million people who saw the final episode of M\*A\*S\*H in 1983, but the tally shows our love for sports entertainment.[1] According to the gaming industry, Nintendo sold 600,000 Wiis in the first eight days they were available in America.[2] TVs, MP3s, CDs, DVDs, and video games dominate our culture.[3] Add the time, energy, and resources that Americans devote to boating, golfing, fishing, and partying, and a startling picture of our devotion to entertainment begins to emerge. Neil Tseng observes, "Over the past half-century, the increase in incomes and decline in hours worked have allowed American consumers to enjoy more leisure time and increase their spending on entertainment. In 2000, spending on entertainment by American consumers totaled approximately $203 billion, almost 3 times the amount that Americans spent on education."[4]

---

[1] Associated Press, "Record 97.5 Million Watch Super Bowl XLII," *msnbc.com*, February 4, 2008, http://msnbc.com/id/22992189. Most readers will profit from skipping the footnotes while reading the main text. The footnotes provide supporting documentation and more thorough argumentation for those who intend additional research.

[2] Reuters, "Nintendo Wii U.S. Sales Top Sony's PS3," *msnbc.com*, December 8, 2006, http://www.msnbc.msn.com/id/16115967; accessed 6 February 2008.

[3] Headlines like these abound: " 'Grand Theft Auto IV' Beats 'Iron Man' by $300 Million" (Associated Press, *foxnews.com*, May 9, 2008, http://www.foxnews.com/story/0,2933,354711,00.html; accessed 12 May 2008). This tally includes only the first week of sales of each. Grand Theft Auto grossed $500 million.

[4] "Expenditures on Entertainment," U.S. Department of Labor, Bureau of Labor Statistics, *Consumer Expenditure Survey Anthology, 2003*, 73, http://www.bls.gov/cex/

The rapid development and widespread use of new entertainment technologies has disoriented many of us as Christians. We have a vague uneasiness concerning the amusements of our age, but even pastors wonder how to address the topic without becoming either reactionary or indifferent. The answer to our confusion is the same today as it has been in every age—we must discern the mind of God from His Word. And we have full assurance that this Word is sufficient to teach us all that is necessary for godly living.

When Solomon wrote Ecclesiastes, he knew nothing about the many favored forms of modern entertainment. Some of our ordinary amusements would have astonished the ancient mind. Yet the wisdom that Solomon applied in his day still addresses our current entertainment choices. The Scriptures provide principles so that each of us may walk rightly in his choice of entertainment.

No one on earth thought as widely and deeply or probed life as fully as Solomon. In investigating every kind of human activity, Solomon concluded that all earthly pursuits were vain in themselves. His conclusion—"fear God, and keep his commandments"— serves as more than a capstone on a book that details one man's exploration of human activity. It grants liberating insight into the purpose of humanity, and it permits legitimate, diverse expressions of joy.

We still face the same traps of life that Solomon faced. We can respond to the evil of our age by withdrawing from all entertainments. We may attempt to shield ourselves from moral defilement by rejecting pleasure or by narrowing our definition of what constitutes righteous joy. We could even seek piety through a Chris-

anthology/csxanth10.pdf. This article breaks entertainment down by categories, age groups, and per-capita expenditures.

tianized Stoicism. However, Solomon tested that philosophy and recognized its emptiness (Eccles. 2:12–23).

On the other hand, we could immerse ourselves in the pleasures of our age and ridicule every attempt to restrict our amusement choices. This mindset exalts a distorted form of Christian liberty. We could take an even more extreme position and reject the application of authoritative moral principles at all. This position claims that we attain true goodness through a Christianized hedonism.[5] Solomon evaluated that philosophy and demonstrated its vanity as well (Eccles. 2:1–12).

"Let us hear the conclusion of the whole matter: Fear God, and keep his commandments: for this is the whole duty of man" (Eccles. 12:13). Solomon did not repudiate the life-diversity that he had previously explored. Rather, he affirmed that we are free to act spontaneously and joyfully as long as we operate within the moral parameters of God's commands. This means that we fulfill our duty toward God not in a rigid pursuit of self-fashioned, self-defined piety but in a submissive will. Our minds should revel in God's creative mind and should rejoice in the power of choice that He has given to humanity. We fulfill our duty toward God not in a cavalier attitude toward life and its activities but in a righteous fear of His holiness and judgment.

It is not our duty to study endlessly, to wear ourselves out physically, or to prostrate ourselves incessantly. But it is also not our liberty to please ourselves thoughtlessly, to live carelessly, or to glut ourselves insatiably. Yet we tend to rush to extremes of thought in our responsibility toward God. Only through a careful consideration of God's thoughts on entertainment can we live freely and

---

[5]The term *Christianized hedonism* as it appears in this paper has no reference to recent works by John Piper. Rather, it addresses a philosophy akin to classical Greek hedonism.

rightly in this realm. This is God's ultimate design—freedom and righteousness, freedom in righteousness, and righteous freedom. From Genesis onward, the Scriptures teach that we are most truly free when we are most righteous.[6]

## DEFINITION

In order to get our bearings, it is crucial that we address the same topic. In order to do this, we must define our key term, *entertainment*.

Although an authoritative definition of entertainment may not be possible, the following observations help to refine a definition to the point of reasonable clarity. **Entertainment is any action that is *calculated* to provide diversion, pleasure, interest, and amusement.**[7] As such, it is the deliberate filling of otherwise idle times with things that amuse,[8] bring diversion, stimulate interest, or generate pleasure.[9] It is also that toward which people often gravitate when they are not providing for the necessities of life. Of all of man's activities, entertainment is one that is designed primarily for pleasure. One could say that the purpose of entertain-

---

[6]See chapter 3 below.

[7]Richard Kraus defines *recreation* by the following elements: "activity . . . as contrasted to sheer idleness or complete rest," diversity of form, voluntary involvement, internal motivation, a recreational state of mind, and the potential for constructive results. *Recreation and Leisure in Modern Society* (New York: Appleton-Century-Crofts, 1971), 261–62.

[8]*Amusement* in this context pertains to the more common usage rather than the etymological or archaic ones. Etymologically, the word comes from *a* (either intensive or adversative) + *muse* (to stare or stare stupidly). Ironically, its earliest uses in the English language mean exactly opposite of its later usage. In the middle of its history the word meant either the active engagement of the mind or the idleness of the mind. Commonly the word simply means something that entertains or pleases. This paper uses the word in the last, non-depreciatory sense.

[9]According to Kraus, "Aristotle regarded leisure as 'a state of being in which activity is performed for its own sake.' It was sharply contrasted with work, or purposeful action" (254).

ment contrasts with other human activities in that it centers on pleasure.[10]

When we talk about entertainment, we usually mean the commercial entertainment industry. This commercial entertainment can be public (theaters, concerts, sports arenas) or private (television, radio). But entertainment also includes non-commercial forms such as participating in sports, games, and hobbies. All of these types of entertainment share common elements that lead to our definition.

*Entertainment* is not strictly synonymous with *pleasure*, though it certainly produces pleasure. *Entertainment* is also not synonymous with the verb *to amuse*. An activity can be amusing or pleasing even when it is not itself entertainment. Some people find their work pleasurable, yet no one considers it to be entertainment. Entertainment goes beyond a mere receiving *of* pleasure to a deliberate reaching *for* pleasure. It involves deliberate or intentional diversion. In addition, *entertainment* cannot be equated strictly with *play*. Play is a single form of entertainment. According to Roger Caillois, *play* adds unproductiveness and uncertainty to an action.[11] Entertainment is the broader category.

Furthermore, *entertainment* is not simply an activity that rests the mind, since many forms of leisure exercise the mind to some extent. For example, in arguing the dangers of television, video games, and music, some writers exaggerate the mental atrophy that

---

[10]This definition has the merit of identifying a class of actions (diversion, pleasure) while providing differentiation within the class by excluding sleep and absolute idleness. Its breadth is sufficient to encompass those actions that all agree to be entertainment without over-broadening to the point of meaninglessness. It incorporates all four broad categories of entertainment mentioned in the following paragraph (commercial and non-commercial forms of public and private amusement) without unnecessarily expanding the scope to a point of meaningless inclusiveness.

[11]*Man, Play and Games*, trans. Meyer Barash (n.p.: Free Press of Glencoe, 1958), 10.

occurs. While it is true that these media tend to relax the rational and cognitive processes of the mind (the left hemisphere), they actually tend to strengthen the emotional, subjective, and reactive centers of the brain (the right hemisphere). Coleen Cook observes, "Viewing is a paradox . . . because it does not rest the mind, since it occupies it with imagery, nor does it stimulate the mind, because it impedes the ability to think. The mind is empty, yet filled at the same time."[12] Likewise, Shane Hipps comments, "Images entertain us and return us to the intuitive, right-brain world of an oral culture. In a very basic sense this return to right-brain thinking undermines critical capacities for theological discernment and the faithful interpretation of Scripture. We need the rational left-brain skills to develop coherence and discern meaning in our amorphous culture."[13]

A pejorative definition of entertainment such as "any activity that lacks redeeming purpose or value" can hardly stand. In that case entertainment amounts to an absolute moral, physical, social, mental, and spiritual idleness that Scripture prohibits.[14] In such a case a Christian position on entertainment could be narrowed to a simple command to abstain entirely from any and all forms of it.

## JUSTIFICATION FOR THE DEFINITION

The purpose of this definition is not to assess the legitimacy of specific forms of entertainment at this point. We will evaluate these later against the biblical criteria for pleasure.[15] Instead, the inten-

[12]*All That Glitters* (Chicago: Moody Press, 1992), 215–16.

[13]*The Hidden Power of Electronic Culture: How the Media Shapes Faith, the Gospel, and Church* (Grand Rapids: Zondervan, 2005), 131.

[14]Leland Ryken concurs: "When put into a context of traditional ethical viewpoints, leisure is incompatible with idleness, utilitarianism, and self-abasement." *Work & Leisure in Christian Perspective* (Portland, OR: Multnomah, 1987), 181. Ryken's work is well worth consulting.

[15]See the section below entitled "Biblical Criteria for Evaluating Entertainment."

tionally broad scope of the definition establishes a reasonable clas-
sification of human conduct rather than arbitrarily and unfairly
tightening it. Several additional arguments demonstrate this to be
a valid and constructive definition.

First, this definition is based on broader real usage in the English language.[16] Although the term *entertainment* is slowly moving toward equation with mass entertainment, it still carries the
broader meaning. Second, a search for synonyms of entertainment
confirms the validity of the definition. Synonyms include *amusement, distraction, diversion, hobby*, and *recreation*.[17] Third, in order
to explore the Christian's interaction with entertainment, we must
treat it first in broad terms to create an adequate biblical philosophy, which can then narrow to specific application in any given instance. Since we engage in such wide-ranging and changing forms
of entertainment, restriction of the definition would shield many
or most of our leisure activities from serious evaluation. Such a
restriction would be perilous, since no generation can foresee the
scope and types of entertainment of succeeding generations. One
of my primary intentions is to propose a biblical pattern of evaluation that will aid each reader in discerning good and evil in any
and all forms of entertainment—past, present, and future. Fourth,

---

[16]*Webster's Ninth New Collegiate Dictionary* defines entertainment as "something diverting or engaging." *Webster's Ninth*, s.v. "Entertainment." *The Oxford English Dictionary* cites twelve different meanings—nine of which are obsolete, two of which pertain
to receiving guests, and the remaining one being "the action of occupying (a person's)
attention agreeably; interesting employment; amusement," "that which affords interest
or amusement," or "a public performance or exhibition intended to interest or amuse."
*The Oxford English Dictionary*, s.v. "Entertainment." *The American Heritage Dictionary
of the English Language* defines it as "1. The act of entertaining. 2. The art or field of
entertaining. 3. Something that amuses, pleases, or diverts, especially a performance or
show. 4. The pleasure afforded by being entertained; amusement." *American Heritage
Dictionary*, 4th ed., s.v. "Entertainment."

[17]See, for example, *The New American Roget's College Thesaurus in Dictionary Form*
(New York: The World Publishing Company, 1962), 145; Marc McCutcheon, *Roget's
Super Thesaurus* (Cincinnati: Writer's Digest Books, 1995), 183. While some thesau-
ruses group *leisure* with *entertainment*, it seems best to define *leisure* as discretionary
time that can be used in a variety of different ways, including entertainment.

if we narrow the definition preemptively, we will more likely fall
into one of several extremes. We might assert that entertainment
is wholly impermissible, or we could react negatively toward an
unwarranted constriction of genuine humanity and cast off even
legitimate restraint. Finally, anyone who recognizes the common
basis in commercial and non-commercial public and private entertainments should reject a definition of entertainment that applies
to only one branch.

The definition should be retained as formulated: Entertainment is
any action that is calculated to provide diversion, pleasure, interest, and amusement. [18]

This definition reveals much about our inner man. What we consider to be entertaining bares the true condition of our hearts.
To know what interests, amuses, diverts, and pleases a person is
to know his quality.[19] Bruce C. Daniels observes this well: "Patterns of leisure and recreation are manifestations of a society's core
identity."[20] For the believer the things that are calculated to bring
him pleasure must be things approved by God. This is not to say
that entertainment should be uniform or bland for the Christian.
It is not limited by the artificial standard of human uniformity,
but it must conform to God's own moral character as revealed in
His Word.

---

[18]The definition as formulated here is entirely the composition of the author. It sets
the scope for the remainder of the work. Entertainment is not identical to popular culture, but popular culture is devoted to entertainment. For this reason many books on
the subject of popular culture provide important data for the topic of entertainment.

[19]Although he writes from a humanistic and evolutionary perspective, Charles K.
Brightbill is correct in observing, "Nowhere do we reveal our selves more fully than in
our worship and in our recreation." *Man and Leisure: A Philosophy of Recreation* (Englewood Cliffs, NJ: Prentice-Hall, 1961), 99.

[20]*Puritans at Play: Leisure and Recreation in Colonial New England* (New York: St.
Martin's Press, 1995), xi.

## SUMMARY

The following chapters are designed to provoke serious thought on a complex issue.[21] Abuses of entertainment recur in every generation. We cannot arrive at a detailed biblical answer by asking superficial questions. Too often, Christians seek for pat answers, simplistic fixes, or ill-conceived patches for a problem rather than engaging their minds in careful thought and deep meditation on Scripture. It is incumbent on the pastor and serious student of Scripture to grapple with the topic of entertainment in a methodical fashion. To that end this work will pursue the following course.

This initial chapter has presented an introduction to the issue and has raised awareness of the need for this study. Chapter 2 provides biblical guidelines for avoiding entertainment traps and for evaluating modern entertainment. These guidelines are prone to abuse, however, so chapter 3 surveys the broader biblical data on entertainment. This chapter contends that some forms of entertainment are natural and good. In one sense the third chapter forms the backbone of the work; however, the detail and complexity of its argument make it more difficult reading. Chapter 4 probes some common mistakes in creating personal standards for entertainment. It shows how an overemphasis on only a portion of biblical data can lead to extremes in our thinking. The article concludes with several important test cases that show how the preceding philosophy and guidelines square with both biblical examples and current application.

---

[21]Much of what we find on the Christian's use of leisure is too cursory to be substantially valuable. For example, see Charles R. Swindoll, *Leisure: Having Fun Is Serious Business* (Portland, OR: Multnomah, 1981).

# 2

## DISCERNING THE RIGHT APPLICATION OF ENTERTAINMENT TODAY

### TRAPS OF ENTERTAINMENT

Although God's Word permits righteous entertainment,[1] we must act wisely in our use of diversions. Prior to the Fall man could not have abused pleasure; he had no sinful inclinations that warped his thinking and acting. But now he has a tendency toward unwise amusement choices.[2] Instead of serving its natural purpose—to provide righteous pleasure and interest while stimulating creativity —entertainment now sets snares for the unwary. We face four basic traps in our entertainment choices: addiction, distraction, escapism, and a contradiction of truth. The positive principles that help us avoid these traps will follow in the section on biblical criteria for evaluating entertainment choices.

### Excess and Addiction

Amusement lays its first trap in excess and addiction. We all find ourselves prone to push even good things to destructive extremes. Although moral virtues know no limitations, we can carry most individual acts to an extreme. For instance, food is essential to life, but both biblical injunction and experience teach us that excessive use of food (gluttony) produces negative consequences. Excess dis-

---

[1] See a defense of this statement below in chapter 3, "A Biblical Guide to Entertainment."

[2] "Critics are right to worry about the potential influence 'the market-driven, therapeutic, narcissistic and entertainment-oriented culture' can have on church and society. We should not fall prey to a naïve consumption of popular culture without critical Christian appraisal." William D. Romanowski, *Eyes Wide Open: Looking for God in Popular Culture* (Grand Rapids: Brazos Press, 2001), 13.

torts God's intention. Work is good; but if a person directs all his energy and attention toward a single responsibility, he can destroy himself, his family, and his ministry. We know this is true since God established the Sabbath rest as part of His plan. It brought physical rest to the people and the land, and it gave them time for spiritual refreshment and renewal. Jesus acknowledged this to be true and drew His disciples apart temporarily for rest (Mark 6:30–32). Work, however, is less seductive than amusement. Under the curse, work burdens mankind heavily. It produces an intense desire for reprieve or escape, but entertainment has no such constraint. It seems to offer the reprieve that people seek. It addicts them to a false sense of freedom and release. It creates an insatiable desire for diversion. The very gift of rest that God gave for refreshment can turn quickly into a plague of overindulgence.

Most of us have experienced this trap firsthand in our entertainment. Even assuming that we engage only in that which is morally defensible, amusement can rapidly encroach on our time. Instead of using entertainment for periodic refreshment, we find ourselves drawn to it—craving its diversion on a long-term basis. When we cannot go a week without playing that game, or when we cannot miss any episode of our favorite show, we demonstrate an unhealthy addiction to entertainment. Quentin J. Schultze observes, "Perhaps the most chilling condemnation of contemporary television is the seemingly insatiable appetite it creates for amusement of all kinds without regard for social or moral benefits."[3] Satan often uses this "insatiable appetite" to slip us increasing doses of sin. Schultze continues, "The desire to know how a story ends frequently gets in the way of making discerning judgments about whether a story

---

[3]*Redeeming Television: How TV Changes Christians—How Christians Can Change TV* (Downers Grove, IL: InterVarsity, 1992), 41.

is worthwhile."[4] Most of us, if we are honest, will admit that some of our favorite entertainments have become increasingly crass, immoral, and blasphemous over time. But we have been ensnared by addiction, and sin invades our souls through the open door of our obsession with amusement.

Addiction often grows slowly. We golf once a month, then every other week, then pore over golf magazines in any downtime we have. We watch three hours of television a week, then eight, then twenty. The tendency to absorb disproportionate amounts of our time makes entertainment dangerous for us. We must avoid this first snare through regular, conscious evaluation of our use of time.

**Distraction**
Earthly pleasure leads to a second trap of distraction. Diversion is an appropriate purpose of amusement. God did not intend for us to be permanently fixated on any one human activity. When it is coupled with excess, however, distraction becomes spiritually and morally paralyzing. Michel de Montaigne illustrated this point when he wrote, "Variation ever relieves, dissolves, and dissipates. . . . Shifting place, business, and company, I secure myself in the crowd of other thoughts and fancies, where it loses my trace, and I escape. . . . A little thing will turn and divert us, because a little thing holds us. We do not much consider subjects in gross and singly; they are little and superficial circumstances or images that touch us."[5] Montaigne used amusement to escape pain, guilt, much-needed introspection, and, ultimately, God. Excessive entertainment may be one of the chief enemies of spiritual meditation. Robert G. DeMoss Jr. emphasizes this point: "*Distraction* promises me a fast-paced, thrill-a-minute experience of fun and excitement

[4]Ibid., 41–42.
[5]*The Essays of Montaigne*, trans. Charles Cotton, ed. W. Carew Hazlitt (New York: A. L. Burt, n.d.), 2:303–4.

but ultimately prevents me from going deeper in my relationships with my family, my friends, and most importantly with God."[6]

Both entertainment and meditation aim for the same objective through different means. Both strive to produce rest and to provide diversion. Moreover, God created both to exist. However, entertainment provides an easier, more immediate, tangible pleasure that often drowns out meditation. It substitutes an important but lesser physical rest for a more important spiritual and physical rest. In entertainment a person can become too busy "relaxing" to find ultimate rest. He views scriptural reflection and deliberation as hard work—too hard to engage in after a long day of other responsibilities. God never intended for delight in the physical pleasures He created to supplant communion with Himself. In the original state of man, the two were complementary, not contradictory. For the believer they must remain so.

As a corollary to distraction, entertainment ensnares people in its worthlessness. I do not use *worthlessness* to indicate a total lack of value, but a deficiency in comparative value. Entertainment has real value, especially when the believer finds pleasure, amusement, and merit in something that is or reveals truth; but many forms of entertainment fall short of the superior value obtained in moral virtues. A problem arises in what entertains humanity. Much of the mass-entertainment industry feeds mankind on empty husks that do not really bring the long-term, promised pleasure. Worse, society often finds real amusement in these husks. It ascribes profound significance and abiding value to activities that have little worth. Entertainment should be constructive rather than worthless or destructive. Even secular writers complain about people's misusing leisure in ways that encourage self-destruction of culture.

---

[6]*TV: The Great Escape! Life-Changing Stories from Those Who Dared to Take Control* (Wheaton: Crossway, 2001), 97.

"If people engage in creative and constructive activities during their leisure, civilization is advanced; if they indulge in useless and destructive activities, the social order deteriorates and progress is retarded."[7] He also demonstrates that the humanistic hope for people to use their increasing leisure time wisely has not borne good fruit in practice. As leisure has increased, commercial entertainments have as well. They sap the productive energy of a person without improving him mentally, socially, physically, or spiritually. Neumeyer's response to this situation is a typically humanistic one: Educate people to use their leisure more effectively.[8] However, the problem resides in the will of man, not his mind.

As believers, we should cultivate an acute awareness of this trap. Too often we attach ourselves devotedly to a particular hobby, music form, or television program. We are willing to set aside the discipling of our children, the caring for our household, the building up of our neighbors, and the preparing of our hearts to know God in favor of things that have lesser value. Scripture does not prohibit our entertainment, but it does prohibit self-gratification while neglecting responsibility. For example, in Isaiah 58:13 God does not condemn the people's seeking of pleasure. He condemns their seeking of pleasure to the neglect of the Sabbath day. When they neglected their responsibility to obey God in favor of pursuing lesser things, their actions became sin. We, too, must avoid this tendency to misuse entertainment in a manner that distracts us from God's will.

### Escapism

Entertainment sometimes serves to feed escapism that leads people away from God. Whereas the former trap of distraction was incidental, the trap of escapism is intentional. We can use amusement

---

[7]Martin H. and Esther S. Neumeyer, *Leisure and Recreation: A Study of Leisure and Recreation in Their Sociological Aspects* (New York: A. S. Barnes, 1949), 13.

[8]Ibid., 16.

to drown out truth. Life under the curse brings toil, suffering, misery, and despair to the heart of man. Pleasure offers a temporary escape from reality. Neumeyer and Neumeyer observe, "Eventual leisure has been the dream of the human race. The world has longed for rest and for freedom from want and the struggle for existence."[9] When a person watches television, plays games, listens to music, enjoys sports, or engages in a hobby, he suspends momentarily the sorrow, pain, and pressure that his conscience and his body experience. Though God provided entertainment for individuals to enjoy Him through creation, they often use entertainment to avoid Him in creation. People hide themselves among the trees of their amusements just as Adam and Eve hid themselves from the presence of God.

People also try to escape the effects of the curse by their own means. God offers the only real escape from sin and its bondage through faith in Jesus Christ, but that escape appears distant. It requires passing through the veil of death. It requires a life lived under the curse, not immune to the pain and suffering that surrounds us. Entertainment claims to grant immediate escape from the curse. People seek pleasure; entertainment obliges. People desire freedom from responsibility, from work, and from their own thoughts; entertainment rushes in to give them that illusory freedom. Entertainment ensnares them in the trap of escapism by drowning out reality, but it cannot replace reality. In that sense entertainment serves as a philosophical fraud for those who do not discern the limitations of its power. It plays the part of a painkiller rather than that of a surgeon. It dulls sensation while allowing the root problem to run unchecked. Accordingly, the believer should use entertainment to enjoy the goodness of God rather than to run from Him. Whenever we use entertainment to circumvent our re-

---

[9]Ibid., 14.

sponsibility, we find ourselves trapped by amusement. When we use entertainment to escape God, to avoid studying His Word, or to evade prayer, we succumb to the spirit of our age.

## Contradiction of Truth

The fourth trap of entertainment is a contradiction of truth. Some entertainment is inherently sinful in its defiance of the parameters that God has already set for man. In the process of amusing ourselves, we can create an alternative reality that rejects truth. As Paul Borgman notes, "Television's tales are an incomplete gospel of good deeds and happy endings, because they do not clearly express our need for God or God's willingness to help."[10] Yet as Christ's parables demonstrate, even fiction has value when it illustrates and complements the truth. Fiction itself is not a contradiction of truth. It reflects our God-given use of imagination. If our fiction contradicts His moral order, if it encourages people to believe ideas contrary to the truth, it crosses the line from illustration to opposition.

For instance, there is an important difference between certain children's fables that teach a biblically sound, moral point and the average cartoon today.[11] Several recent animations teach us that parents need to let children do as they wish. It is the parent who must repent of his overly restrictive attitude rather than the juvenile who must repent of his prodigality. This is an inversion of God's moral order. Borgman approves of the selective use of television since in the average television plot "happiness usually depends on victory over some form of oppression."[12] This is true as

---

[10] *TV: Friend or Foe?* (Elgin, IL: David C. Cook, 1979), 91.

[11] This is not to imply that all fables are worthwhile reading. Harold Schechter documents the fact that many fables and fairy tales present appalling violence and inhumanity. *Savage Pastimes: A Cultural History of Violent Entertainment* (New York: St. Martin's Press, 2005), 11–13.

[12] *TV*, 89–90.

long as the "oppression" in view is something God would define to be oppression. Victory over crime, over interpersonal conflict, over racial tension accurately reflects God's intent for man. Unfortunately, television, video games, and movies increasingly depict righteousness as oppression. Our culture seeks victory over the intolerance of biblical sexual restraint, and it advocates silencing the oppressiveness of Christ-centered religion. This means that we have to evaluate our entertainment choices very carefully. Some depict God's moral order. Some contradict that order. We can affirm the former but must reject the latter.

This trap is especially perilous to the believer, since it packages sin as frivolous, fun, or inconsequential. From the beginning Satan has understood that he can wear down the righteous resistance of God's people by minimizing sin's gravity. His voice speaks in the seductiveness of immoral entertainment. Just as he once contradicted God's Word, "Ye shall not surely die," he now claims, "You shall not surely be defiled." We cannot yield to sin packaged as pleasure. When we see wrong philosophy being taught to our children, we must address it with them. We cannot be so caught up in entertainment that we fail to instruct them in the truth. If our pursuit of diversion, pleasure, or amusement contradicts God's definition of righteous pleasure, then we must abandon our own way in obedience to the Lord.

## BIBLICAL CRITERIA FOR EVALUATING ENTERTAINMENT
We must not respond to these entertainment traps with moral paralysis that refuses to do anything, moral terror that rejects the good God has created, or moral haughtiness that establishes our own preference as the authoritative standard. Likewise, we must not minimize the seriousness of the issue or deny the consequences of wrong choices. We must turn to Scripture for moral guidelines.

This process of turning to Scripture applies in every generation. A work produced by Puritan ministers in 1726, titled *A Serious Address to Those Who Unnecessarily Frequent the Tavern . . .* , provides insight into criteria used by previous generations of believers. Daniels cites this document: " 'Harmless recreation,' they argued, should 'be governed by reason and virtue,' be 'convenient, sparing, prudent,' 'give place to business,' 'observe proper rules,' 'subserve religion,' and 'minister to the Glory of God.' "[13] Robert Lee provides a similar list of criteria for appropriate entertainment: "There is evidence enough to indicate that the Puritans were not opposed to diversion and recreation, provided it was truly refreshing, was not a waste of time, was not done in excess, and was not immoral or sensual."[14]

Several crucial thoughts stem from these observations. First, the Christian *must* turn to Scripture. We may not respond to our own spiritual ignorance with apathy. We cannot be idle. We cannot absolve ourselves of the responsibility to search out God's will in this area. Remember Solomon's words: "Rejoice, O young man, in thy youth; and let thy heart cheer thee in the days of thy youth, and walk in the ways of thine heart, and in the sight of thine eyes: *but know thou, that for all these things God will bring thee into judgment*" (Eccles. 11:9). The awareness that God will judge all our deeds should motivate us to be the best-informed people on the earth. Luke 12:47–48 reminds us that ignorance is not an excuse. While the ignorant sinner may experience slightly less severe consequences, he will still suffer the punishment due his crime (Prov. 22:3). Proverbs 1:32 confirms that "the waywardness of the naïve will kill them" (NASB). Moreover, it is unlikely that willful ignorance will reduce culpability at all (Prov. 1:22). If anything,

---

[13] Cited in *Puritans at Play*, 19.

[14] *Religion and Leisure in America: A Study in Four Dimensions* (New York: Abingdon, 1964), 163.

willful ignorance adds additional sin. God gave His Word to mankind to make the simple wise (Ps. 19:7). Its testimony calls men to understanding (Prov. 8:5–6, 9:4). Paul encourages wisdom in righteousness and simplicity in evil, and he notes that the naïve have a greater susceptibility to deception and overthrow by false teachers (Rom. 16:18–19). Scripture commands us to know what is right and to do it.

Second, we must turn *to Scripture*. Although God's Word permits righteous entertainment, we are not free to choose and act however we wish. Too often Christians "make decisions like unbelievers, and usually they have no concept that this is how they live. Nowhere is this more apparent than in the area of amusement. If this is the case, it may be because few Christians have ever thought deeply on the subject of entertainment, and even fewer understand the danger."[15] It is disturbing to observe that in our culture conservative as well as liberal arguments rest so heavily on personal opinion.[16] Proponents of morality sink to the same subjectivity that

---

[15]Gary Gilley, *This Little Church Went to Market: Is the Modern Church Reaching Out or Selling Out?* (Webster, NY: Evangelical Press USA, 2005), 77–78. Schultze concurs: "My own surveys of adolescent and adult viewing by Christians suggest that they implicitly use the same standards of the overall population" (*Redeeming Television*, 102). Unfortunately, Schultze fails to develop explicitly biblical criteria in his own commentary on television. Instead he lists innovation, quality of performance, fittingness, universality of theme, traditional aesthetic merits, and redemptiveness as his criteria (112–25). Of these criteria only "redemptiveness" has any real scriptural basis. Schultze has to qualify his own criteria so extensively that they do not ring true as objective standards of right and wrong. These criteria may serve as a secondary line of defense and evaluation that will help the believer decide among biblically acceptable options, but they do not define biblically acceptable options.

[16]See the opposing viewpoints represented in William Barbour, ed. *Mass Media: Opposing Viewpoints* (n.p.: Greenhaven Press, 1994). A clear demonstration of this subjectivity appears in Tipper Gore, *Raising PG Kids in an X-Rated Society* (Nashville: Abingdon, 1987). While she rejects the extreme violence and sexuality of our present culture, she has no viable alternative other than her own opinion: "No one should want a return to the sexual hypocrisy of the 1950s, which was unrealistic and often repressive. But the pendulum has swung too far in our time" (98–99). See also her approval of rock music (17, 144) and MTV (18) in their less extreme forms. As Christians, we wonder who gets to define "too far."

their opponents use. Pragmatism rules the day. Some argue that entertainment is the source of all ills and must be contained; others argue that it is the source of progress and must be unbridled. Both try to make a statistical and logical case apart from any external, objective standard. Christians must base their decisions on something far greater than personal opinion. We must know the divine Word that is the basis of judgment. God will not judge our works by our opinions. It is foolish, then, for us to spend our time trying to justify our entertainment choices by any standard other than Scripture. God's Word is the source of our moral guidelines.

Third, we must turn to Scripture for moral *guidelines*. God deals graciously with us in areas of natural humanity warped by the fall. He does not prohibit what He created to be legitimate. The only exceptions to this principle in Genesis are the access to the tree of the knowledge of good and evil (Gen. 3:23–24), access to the tree of life (Gen. 3:22–24), and direct communion with God face-to-face (inferred from Gen. 1:28–29; 2:16–17; 3:8–19 and the diminishing references to direct communication thereafter). Instead He limits the now-sinful tendencies of mankind. There are some facets of humanity that are philosophically good in reference to the original creation but are practically bad in some specific applications. Rather than banning the whole, God forbids only that which violates His original principles and intent. For example, in each of the following instances, natural humanity received and retains some freedom to act. But after the Fall man also received and retains specific limitations on these freedoms: dominion (Gen. 1:26, 28), sexuality (Gen. 1:28), eating (Gen. 1:29), productivity (Gen. 2:15), and nakedness (Gen. 2:25).

The following guidelines help us to sift our entertainment through a biblical grid and retain that which conforms to God's intended purpose.[17] In order to use entertainment in a Christ-honoring fashion, the Christian must follow them:

- Pursue conformity to Christ.

- Approve beauty and excellence.

- Guard personal contentment.

- Reject earthly and sensual domination.

- Test the means and reality of knowledge.

- Maintain extensive personal labor.

- Retain scripturally directed and sensible priorities.

- Have a godly purposefulness in activity.

- Exclude all that defiles purity.

- Build edifying relationships.

- Exhibit discerning wisdom and hold fast to truth.

## Pursue Conformity to Christ

In a sense all biblical criteria concerning entertainment derive from the overarching criterion of conformity. *Conformity* is agreement, harmony, and correspondence in character, conduct, form, or manner. In addressing conformity, our minds naturally ask the question, "Conformity to what?" The New Testament answers that question clearly in four passages.[18]

---

[17]Rather than creating a dubious and debatable hierarchy of these principles, this work simply cites each principle (other than the overarching principle of conformity) in indiscriminate order. Any such list of biblical criteria is by necessity representative rather than comprehensive. The reader may discern in Scripture additional criteria that follow the same pattern established here.

[18]The first two passages use συμμορφόω. This word normally describes conformity in essential quality. The second two use συσχηματίζω, which normally describes a likeness in shape or accidental quality.

For whom he did foreknow, he also did predestinate to be conformed **to the image of his Son**, that he might be the firstborn among many brethren. (Rom. 8:29)

Who shall change our vile body, that it may be fashioned **like unto his glorious body**, according to the working whereby he is able even to subdue all things unto himself. (Phil. 3:21)

And be **not** conformed **to this world**: but be ye transformed by the renewing of your mind, that ye may prove what is that good, and acceptable, and perfect, will of God. (Rom. 12:2)

As obedient children, **not** fashioning yourselves **according to the former lusts** in your ignorance. But as he which hath called you is holy, so be ye holy in all manner of conversation; because it is written, Be ye holy; for I am holy. (1 Pet. 1:14–16)

The first two verses show us that God destines believers to conform to the image of the Son and to the likeness of His glorious body. If the believer's essential qualities will be conformed to the image of Jesus Christ one day, then he should not deliberately conform to the essence of the world now. The second two verses argue the need for the believer to look like and be like God in conduct and character. Both sets have bearing on the Christian's use of entertainment. Both raise the question, "Does this amusement preserve or restore the image of God in humanity and imitate His character, or does it retain the marred aspects of the image and imitate the world?" Before discussing further the criteria for evaluating entertainment, the believer must acknowledge the need for conformity to the right Person and the right standard.

We are conformists by nature. Scripture assumes that we will look like the world or like God (Rom. 12:1–2). We must imitate. Each generation faces the same desire to be different, to do its own thing, to be rugged individualists—by looking exactly like everyone else in its generation. Children wish to be unique by wearing the same clothes that their peers are wearing. Adults express their individuality by chasing the same homes, cars, vacations, and business that millions of other adults are chasing. The pursuit of novelty ultimately results in frustration, since people must imitate. The only question concerns *what* one will imitate. God calls His children to imitate Him (Eph. 5:1; 1 Thess. 1:6); the world calls believers to imitate it (3 John 11). By examining the moral character of God and matching our actions to that character, we can enjoy diversion, pleasure, and amusement that are wholesome and consonant with God's will. Due to the sinfulness of humanity, we either actively conform ourselves to the right standard, or we will conform to the vanity of this world.

We could also express the criterion of conformity in terms of *truth*. Ultimately when the Christian seeks conformity, he seeks accord with God's standard of truth. *Truth* does not address merely the factuality of a person or event. It includes a right perspective of that person or event. Truth does not address whether or not immorality, violence, slander, and other forms of evil ever occur in the historical sense. Rather it discusses whether those actions and philosophies conform to God's standard of what is true and right. In other words, when a person conforms his life to the world, is he really conforming himself to truth? The world claims that sexual license, the expression of personal anger in violent acts, instant gratification of all wishes, and collective tolerance are "true." It insists that "man is the measure of all things" and that he will never experience the judgment of a higher power. The Christian has every right to ask, "Are these claims true?" His conclusion concerning their truthfulness depends on his own conformity to God's standard of truth, which preexists and preempts all human definitions. Ultimately we must ask, "Does this entertainment make me more or less like Christ?"

## Approve Beauty and Excellence

When the believer revisits the question, "Why does this amuse or entertain me?" he should be able to provide a response consonant with beauty. Few verses communicate this principle as simply and powerfully as Philippians 4:8: "Finally, brethren, whatsoever things are true, whatsoever things are honest, whatsoever things are just, whatsoever things are pure, whatsoever things are lovely, whatsoever things are of good report; if there be any virtue, and if there be any praise, think on these things." The verse commands man's focused attention on that which is naturally and morally noble. In particular the term *honest* addresses that which is honorable or venerable, and *lovely* pertains to that which is pleasing and acceptable. Yet these must be held to be honorable and lovely within a context of truth, rightness, and purity. In other words, the verse will not allow an individual to define the revered and lovely thing by his own degraded opinion. Kenneth A. Myers rightly observes, "Paul does not say that we should reflect on what we *think* is lovely, or whatever we *feel* is admirable. We are to give sustained attention to whatever is *objectively* true and noble and right."[19]

As tarnished as society is becoming, people still do not visit the city dump for their family vacations. Everyone appreciates natural beauty, and that appreciation is God-given. God Himself delights in and commends the beauty in the garments of the priests (Exod. 28:2, 40), the beauty of human appearance (1 Sam. 16:12; 25:3),

[19] *All God's Children and Blue Suede Shoes: Christians & Popular Culture* (Wheaton, IL: Crossway, 1989), 98.

24

the beauty of gems and gold ornamentation (2 Chron. 3:6; Ezra 7:7), the beauty of geographic or topographic location (Ps. 48:2), the beauty of timeliness and all of creation (Eccles. 3:11; Isa. 28:5), the beauty of clothing and jewelry (used figuratively of Jerusalem in Isa. 52:1; see also Ezek. 7:20; 16:12–14), and the beauty of trees (used figuratively in Ezek. 31:8 and Hosea 14:6). He also ascribes beauty to intangible things such as holiness (1 Chron. 16:29; 2 Chron. 20:21; Ps. 29:2), majesty and dignity (Job 40:10), and His own person (Ps. 50:2).

No one has to instruct an observer on the art of appreciation when he sees the Grand Canyon, the Rocky Mountains, Niagara Falls, or white sand beside a crystal-green ocean. Similarly, our entertainment should elevate rather than degrade things of beauty. "To the contemporary mind, goodness and beauty are often boring and unstimulating."[20] Perverting the sanctity and blessing of marriage, mocking the tender love of parent-child relationships, or encouraging barbarism, violence, and inhumanity does not coincide with beauty.[21] The periodic hand-wringing that goes on in the media indicates an awareness that something is out of joint. People intuitively know the ugliness of their actions. Nonetheless, after a time of respectable self-flagellation, they will return to the airing of the same ugly programs. Tolkien illustrates this paradox in the misery of Gollum: "He hated and loved [the ring], as he hated

---

[20]Richard Winter, *Still Bored in a Culture of Entertainment: Rediscovering Passion & Wonder* (Downers Grove, IL: InterVarsity, 2002), 38.

[21]In a work devoted to exploring human amusement with violence, Harold Schechter observes that moralists in every generation approve the past and decry the present forms of violent entertainment. See *Savage Pastimes*, 118–27. He documents the carnival atmosphere at public executions in the Middle Ages, the rise of dime novels in the 1800s, and the present infatuation with violent movies and video games. He is correct factually, but he wrongly concludes that inhumanity and gratuitous violence should be acceptable entertainment. Christians do not weigh the rightness of present actions against their acceptability in the past. We weigh our present choices against an eternal standard.

and loved himself."[22] We often acknowledge the ugliness of an act while refusing to abandon it in its ugliness. Many in modern culture have a greater concern for cleaning up oil spills, leaving virgin forests intact, and protecting wildflowers than they do for cleaning up the spilling of blood, leaving virgin young minds intact, and protecting innocence. They see natural beauty but will not recognize moral beauty. The believer must not be so. On the authority of Scripture, we should ask, "Is this entertainment consistent with true beauty?"[23]

This involves the additional criterion of excellence. The wisdom books of Scripture address excellence with favor.[24] Although the topics of wisdom range widely, all that is noble, pure, and wise falls into the category of excellence (Prov. 8:6; 22:20). Popular entertainment in particular often fails this test. Popular entertainment not only rejects the objective standards of Scripture, it even denies the objective standards of beauty recognized in human high culture.[25]

The believer possesses a new life of moral excellence in Christ (2 Pet. 1:3–9).

---

[22]J. R. R. Tolkien, *The Fellowship of the Ring* (1959; reprint, Boston: Houghton Mifflin, 1991), 54.

[23]T. M. Moore lists beauty, goodness, and truth as the three basic criteria that the believer should use to evaluate his culture. *Redeeming Pop Culture: A Kingdom Approach* (Phillipsburg, NJ: P&R, 2003), 82. The work provides some philosophical points, but the author's misinterpretation of the Christian's responsibility to "address, engage, and take captive the popular culture of our day for the purposes of Christ and His kingdom" due to his postmillennial interpretation of eschatology leads to several inferior applications, including the justifying of a believer's listening to rock music (41).

[24]In these few books 27 of 66 total references to *excel / excellence* occur (KJV).

[25]Myers observes that any attempt to confront popular entertainment with objective standards meets hostility and counter-assertions of arrogance (77, 99). Since popularity is the source of virtue in mass entertainment, its imbibers reject any critique as elitist. Roger Scruton provides a defense for high culture in *An Intelligent Person's Guide to Modern Culture* (South Bend: St. Augustine's Press, 2000). Romanowski, however, rejects the notion of a distinction between high and low culture, insisting that it is an artificial creation of elitists (74).

According as his divine power hath given unto us all things that pertain unto life and godliness, through the knowledge of him that hath called us to glory and virtue: whereby are given unto us exceeding great and precious promises: that by these ye might be partakers of the divine nature, having escaped the corruption that is in the world through lust. And beside this, giving all diligence, add to your faith virtue; and to virtue knowledge; and to knowledge temperance; and to temperance patience; and to patience godliness; and to godliness brotherly kindness; and to brotherly kindness charity. For if these things be in you, and abound, they make you that ye shall neither be barren nor unfruitful in the knowledge of our Lord Jesus Christ. But he that lacketh these things is blind, and cannot see afar off, and hath forgotten that he was purged from his old sins.

Having been called from a life of sin by God's own excellence (v. 3) and having been made partakers of the divine nature through this same excellence (v. 4), Christians grow in sanctification by diligently striving for increasingly mature spiritual character (vv. 5–7).[26] On the basis of God's own moral excellence, we must pursue moral excellence in every facet of our lives. We should rightly question, "Does this leisure activity magnify or diminish what is noble and beautiful?"

## Guard Personal Contentment

Entertainment often creates discontent. In fact, some forms of entertainment rely heavily on their ability to generate dissatisfaction in the viewer or participant. Jerry Mander, a commentator from within the television industry, observes, "Advertising exists only to

---

[26]The term *virtue* (ἀρετή), which follows on the heels of faith, describes moral excellence or nobility of character.

purvey what people don't need. Whatever people do need they will find without advertising if it is available. This is so obvious and simple that it continues to stagger my mind that the ad industry has succeeded in muddying the point."[27] Other amusement forms do not deliberately stimulate covetousness but can become wrong for a person who cannot escape the draw of personal dissatisfaction. The Bible encourages a tranquility of spirit and a deep-seated contentment that come from knowing God (Phil. 4:11; Heb. 13:5). This contentment does not tremble at circumstance or perceived material inferiority. Recognizing the sovereignty of God, we can choose to remain untroubled by wants (1 Tim. 6:6–8). Desires may still exist, but the chafing to possess more things or a different lifestyle should not characterize us.

## Reject Earthly and Sensual Domination

God created humanity under no personal authority but Himself. Adam exercised righteous dominion over the earth and all of its creatures (Gen. 1:26, 28). At first he governed his rational faculties and impulses (Gen. 2:16–17, 19–20). He enjoyed the pleasures that God had made without serving his own pleasure. Sin brought enslavement to our carnal desires—an absolute bondage that continues until we experience deliverance by grace through faith in Christ.

We Christians exist in a morally re-ordered state in which our Lord is Jesus Christ. Our appetites and desires no longer rule. Myers commends this truth by noting that Christians "should not become preoccupied with earthly culture of any sort, neither Bach nor Bon Jovi."[28] Scripturally, this truth holds as well. Romans 6:14 admonishes, "For sin shall not have dominion over you: for ye are

---

[27]*Four Arguments for the Elimination of Television* (New York: William Morrow, 1978), 126.

[28]*All God's Children*, 100. He acknowledges the rightful place for entertainment while insisting that the believer cannot be dominated ("preoccupied") by it.

not under the law, but under grace." Paul argues in 1 Corinthians: "All things are lawful unto me, but all things are not expedient: all things are lawful for me, but I will not be brought under the power of any," and "For ye are bought with a price: therefore glorify God in your body, and in your spirit, which are God's" (6:12, 20).[29] Entertainment becomes sinful to us if it exercises dominion over us. All those who deal with teens on a consistent basis have witnessed first-hand the life-dominating power of amusement. When Christian young people are willing to defy their authorities—rejecting their knowledge, experience, wisdom, and God-appointed right—in order to justify and preserve their entertainment, leisure has seized control of the life and has bred sin. When the believer is so possessed by his culture that he rationalizes his participation in its sinful aspects, he demonstrates his bondage to the spirit of his age.

Many writers warn strongly against the dominating influence of entertainment. Kyle Haselden claims, "Mass media will have an integrating effect on our society and perhaps eventually on the world."[30] Neil Postman concurs and believes that future tyrants will use pleasure as a means of controlling the populace just as much

---

[29]Verse 12 begins a new section rather than attaching to the preceding one. Apparently the Corinthian church had caricatured Paul's position on Christian liberty in justifying their fornication; see Charles Hodge, *A Commentary on 1 & 2 Corinthians* (1857; reprint, Avon: The Bath Press, 1994), 102. This church treated immorality as a temporal pleasure, on the same level as eating and drinking, that would eventually pass away without consequence. Paul refutes the misapplication of the principle not by rescinding the principle but by correcting its application. Philosophically, all pleasures as created by God are lawful; practically, not all pleasures bring advantage. Philosophically, all things are lawful; practically, fallen humanity becomes a slave of his desires. Paul addresses human sexuality very delicately yet clearly. Sexual pleasure is lawful, but when the pleasure rules a person to the point of his disregarding God's commands, its purpose is perverted, and it has become sinful. As R. C. H. Lenski observes, "It is pure folly to insist on *the formal right* expressed by the principle and to ignore *the actual advantages or disadvantages* that will result in any given case." *The Interpretation of St. Paul's First and Second Epistles to the Corinthians* (1937; reprint, Peabody, MA: Hendrickson, 1998), 255.

[30]*Morality and the Mass Media* (Nashville: Broadman, 1968), 70.

29

as the Romans used it to appease the masses.[31] Some writers even speak with an apocalyptic warning: "When Americans become too conditioned to telereality, they are in a position to be emotionally manipulated by whoever or whatever controls the TV camera."[32]

Although all amusements have the potential to dominate a person's life, the mass-media entertainments are particularly notorious and effective in wielding this power.[33] They have to be. Mass media are entirely integrated with the commercialism of society. Money is the ultimate objective, regardless of the collateral damage to morality. This creates the need to entertain more boldly and dramatically in order to captivate an audience—to capture a dedicated following that will watch every episode, buy every album, visit every park, or purchase every accessory. In the process the observer or participant in the entertainment can easily become a slave to his own pleasure.[34] Kenneth A. Myers addresses this domination by popular entertainment:

---

[31] *Amusing Ourselves to Death: Public Discourse in the Age of Show Business* (New York: Viking Penguin, 1985), vii–viii, 141.

[32] Cook, *All That Glitters*, 57. See also Jerry Mander's comment: "It was suddenly possible for an entire nation of 200 million people to be spoken to as individuals, one to one, the television set to the person or family, all at once. I was chilled at the thought, realizing that these conditions of television viewing—confusion, unification, isolation, especially when combined with passivity and what I later learned of the effects of implanted imagery—were ideal preconditions for the imposition of autocracy." *Four Arguments*, 27. Mander is a thoroughgoing secularist who ridicules Western religion. He strongly favors mystic, Oriental, and pagan religions. Yet he exhibits acute awareness of the life-dominating power of entertainment.

[33] Mander testifies a personal sense of being used by television rather than using it. He describes watching television as "antilife" due to its dominating effect. Ibid., 159. See also Marshall McLuhan, "American Advertising," in *Mass Culture: The Popular Arts in America*, ed. Bernard Rosenberg and David Manning White (Glencoe, IL: Free Press, 1957), 435–42.

[34] Some will object to this analysis due to the impotence of the medium of entertainment to control a person. One could split philosophical hairs and assert that person is ultimately captive to his own lusts. Two rejoinders justify the point: amusement can facilitate a domination by lusts, and Paul uses the imagery of domination in 1 Cor. 6 when addressing a parallel circumstance of a man's yielding to lusts.

When we arrive, the stage is already set, the lyrics and music written, our lines and our movements already determined. Popular culture has the power to set the pace, the agenda, and the priorities for much of our social and our spiritual existence, without our explicit consent. It requires a great effort not to be mastered by it.[35]

Even if entertainment serves as merely a facilitator of domination by lust, it still warrants careful scrutiny. Malcolm Muggeridge argues,

The media in themselves have no power, any more than nuclear weapons have; both have power only to the extent that they can influence and exploit the weaknesses and the wretchedness of men—their carnality which makes them vulnerable to the pornographer, their greed and vanity which delivers them into the hands of the advertiser, their credulity which makes them so susceptible to the fraudulent prospectuses of ideologues and politicians; above all, their arrogance, which induces them to fall so readily for any agitator or agitation, revolutionary or counter-revolutionary, which brings to their nostrils the acrid scent of power.[36]

Secular sociologists warn against the excessive use of entertainment in a manner that dominates work ethic and social life.[37] How much more astute must the observations of believers be? We have a divine mandate to avoid life-dominating influences that would compete with our one Lord. On the basis of the peril involved in some entertainments, we must ask, "Does this amusement dominate my life?"

---

[35] *All God's Children*, xiv.

[36] *Christ and Media* (Grand Rapids: Eerdmans, 1978), 45.

[37] Neumeyer and Neumeyer, *Leisure*, 13.

## Test the Means and Reality of Knowledge

The study of the means of knowledge and the certainty of knowing seems an unusual member in a list of biblical criteria for entertainment, but the mass media represent themselves as an essential source of knowledge in the present age.[38] Just ask the six o'clock news anchor and Internet news outlet how important they are to an informed citizenry. The manner and content of instruction in mass media often produce moral confusion, a false sense of knowledge, and crippled critical thinking. Neil Postman is particularly scathing in his denunciation of modern entertainment media. He contends that newsmagazines had "a 'language' that denied interconnectedness, proceeded without context, argued the irrelevance of history, explained nothing, and offered fascination in place of complexity and coherence."[39]

Watching a diverting hour-long program on elephants in the African bush gives every observer the sense of having "been there"—of profound awareness, of real perception—even though he has never seen, heard, smelled, or touched an elephant; has never sweat a drop under the African sun; has never ridden one mile into the bush; has never felt the terror of being charged by an angry bull; and has not spent ten years of his life as the naturalist-photographer compiling the footage for that one-hour documentary. The viewer is left with a *sense* of deep comprehension even though the means of his acquiring that knowledge was shallow. As long as we are aware of the limitations of this knowledge, entertainment can serve a useful purpose. If we impart greater merit and reliability to these entertainment media than they possess, we fail the biblical injunction to "prove all things" (1 Thess. 5:21).

[38]One can find this topic under the heading of *epistemology* in philosophy texts.
[39]*Amusing Ourselves*, 77.

Amusement can supplant thought and experience. "It is only with conscious effort and direct participation at one's own speed that words gain any meaning to a reader. Images require nothing of the sort. They only require that your eyes be open. The images enter you and are recorded in your memory whether you think about them or not. They pour into you like fluid into a container."[40] A person can become distant from the firsthand pleasures God has designed for him to experience. He watches romances on television, sitting side-by-side with his wife, rather than experiencing romance himself. He sees people building, exercising, moving, living, and being while he refuses to participate. These observations on a distorted epistemology do not condemn the diversion brought by even mass entertainment, but they should at least caution the believer against assuming a knowledge he does not really possess. And they warn against a predominantly media-oriented means of knowledge.

Non-commercial entertainment fares better in the field of understanding. At least several different forms of knowledge, such as tradition and experience, engage the participant. Even with their advantages over mass media, other amusements have the tendency to neglect the most important source of knowledge—revelation. In a biblical epistemology revelation is the supreme means of knowledge (e.g., 1 Pet. 1:20–21). God has the essential qualities of a perfect scientific observer. He is in all places, at all times, with all comprehension.[41] Moreover, His capacities for thought and reasoning are perfect.

> For my thoughts are not your thoughts, neither are your
> ways my ways, saith the Lord. For as the heavens are higher

---

[40] *Four Arguments*, 204.

[41] His omnipresence appears in Ps. 139:7–12; Prov. 15:3; and Matt. 28:19–20. His omni-temporality occurs in Ps. 90:1–2; John 8:58; Jude 25; and Rev. 1:8. His omniscience appears in Pss. 139:12; 147:5; Prov. 15:11; Matt. 10:29–30; Acts 15:18; and Heb. 4:13.

than the earth, so are my ways higher than your ways, and my thoughts than your thoughts. (Isa. 55:8–9)

O the depth of the riches both of the wisdom and knowledge of God! how unsearchable are his judgments, and his ways past finding out! For who hath known the mind of the Lord? or who hath been his counsellor? (Rom. 11:33–34)

When, in addition, we admit God's capacity for precise, accurate, clear communication, the knowledge obtained from revelation is impressive. Revelation combines the experience, reason, and "tradition" of God and communicates them to man. Amusement has the tendency to drown out revelation, not always by openly contradicting God's Word, but by usurping the time required to hear the mind of God through His Word.

Used properly, entertainment can communicate some truth. It can speak truly—not to say fully—about God, humanity, and the world. Used improperly, it becomes the predominant source of knowledge and standards.[42] Entertainment is capable of illustrating a reality that already exists, but it cannot define or create reality. If entertainment claims a communication of knowledge that it cannot rightfully own, or if it displaces the study of Scripture that is necessary to know God, we have the duty to reject its validity. This criterion asks, "What truth emerges in this entertainment, and how do I know it is true?"

## Maintain Extensive Personal Labor

Laziness, idleness, and atrophy surround modern man. Prior to the industrial age, natural constraints limited our entertainment. One had to eat to survive; one had to work to eat; and one person could

---

[42]"Surveys show that many professing Christians reason like society in general on questions of divorce, abortion, materialism, premarital sex, and other social and moral issues. In a speech to writers one Christian publisher warned that even within Christian circles the biblical thinker is disappearing." Cook, *All that Glitters*, 23.

produce consistently only enough for a few families. Industry removed the last of these constraints. One person can now plow, sow, and harvest massive tracts of land while harnessing the power of irrigation to thwart all but the most extreme droughts and the power of chemicals to prevent pestilence. Factory workers make myriads of mechanical items to save time. Few of us make our own clothes. Few grow our own food. Few build our own houses or make the objects in our own houses. Specialization has increased. Purchasing has increased. And leisure time has risen dramatically. Robert Lee observes, "Although leisure has always been a fringe benefit in the history of mankind, now it is moving into the center of life, threatening to replace work as the basis of culture."[43] People now weigh the quality of life in American culture not by productivity but by play.

In one sense this diversification and freedom provide a pale reflection of the biblical diversity of humanity and the bounty of God's original creation. However, sinful people have not demonstrated a particularly strong tendency to use their time and energies well. Given more leisure time during the days of the Roman Empire, the people turned to bread and circuses. Given more leisure time in the twentieth century, the people turned to . . . bread and circuses. The situation of our society admits great potential for constructive activity or for wasted time. Many forms of entertainment promote the latter. Modern culture virtually deifies amusement. People want shorter hours of work, more vacation days, earlier retirements. Fortuitous investments have the potential to free us from work altogether. Conversely, the Bible encourages industry without discouraging appropriate periods of rest (Rom. 12:11). Entertainment has reached the point that it can, in some instances, directly contradict the Bible. God's Word says, "Slothfulness casteth into a deep sleep; and an idle soul shall suffer hunger" (Prov. 19:15),

---

[43] *Religion and Leisure*, 19.

but modern culture says a person can amuse himself all day and still receive a check from the government. It is hard not to notice in our cities the dilapidated shacks falling apart from neglect yet crowned with multiple satellite dishes. Where entertainment encourages idleness, it defies God's plan for mankind.

> I went by the field of the slothful, and by the vineyard of the man void of understanding; and, lo, it was all grown over with thorns, and nettles had covered the face thereof, and the stone wall thereof was broken down. (Prov. 24:30–31)

> By much slothfulness the building decayeth; and through idleness of the hands the house droppeth through. (Eccles. 10:18)

Even secular writers acknowledge people's need to work. Jay Nash observes, "Contrary to much of our thinking, man longs to struggle—maybe struggle has a bad connotation—but he does love to master, to conquer."[44] Although these writers have no human explanation for the phenomenon, they observe that we must be productive and creative in order to be happy.[45] We must accomplish something useful in order to retain a sense of dignity and worth. The Christian recognizes God-ordained dominion and stewardship in man's desire for industry. The biblical pattern of human industriousness requires that we look carefully at our choices of entertainment and make them conform to God's intent rather than society's mandate. We should not be amused endlessly by things that degrade

---

[44]*Recreation: Pertinent Readings, Guide Posts to the Future* (Dubuque, IA: Wm. C. Brown, 1965), 3. See also his comment, "Leisure alone is not enough to satisfy; neither is work unless it has significance. Recreation and work together make for fullness. To people who do not work, leisure is meaningless" (4).

[45]The absence of creativity and a proper use of energies leads to what Connie O'Conner calls "subjective fatigue." We become morose, bored, frustrated, and tired when we fail to use time constructively. *The Leisure Wasters* (New York: A. S. Barnes, 1966), 89.

constructive activity. Rather, we should choose from among the many entertainments that support human creativity. Most private non-commercial entertainments (especially hobbies) improve a person intellectually, physically, socially, and even aesthetically. We should use sparingly those entertainments (primarily commercial) that relax our activity to a point of uselessness. This criterion asks, "Am I maintaining a right relationship between work and entertainment in my choices of amusement?"

## Retain Scripturally Directed and Sensible Priorities

The criterion of priority means that when we evaluate an action, we should start with Scripture rather than with our opinions. It is impossible for us to determine accurately the merit of a choice if Scripture has not trained our minds to discern good and evil (Heb. 5:11–14).[46] The Bible portrays many individuals who chose an action and only later acknowledged the need for biblical counsel. Ahab chose to fight against Ramoth-gilead and sought counsel of the Lord only when Jehoshaphat strongly urged it (2 Chron. 18). Zedekiah determined to resist Babylon's attack and then sought counsel from Jeremiah (Jer. 21). In both of these instances the leader predetermined the legitimacy of an action and only later sought divine input. This misordering of the process results in confusion. It is probably not incidental that both of these illustrations also show a rejection of biblical counsel when it was given. Those who invert their priorities in the first place are likely to reject later counsel. They have already demonstrated what they value by their ordering of actions. These examples stand in stark contrast to the many instances in which men sought biblical wisdom in the first place and experienced the blessing of God because of it. Our start-

---

[46]The biblical writer's complaint that the people are "dull of hearing" and that they who should be mature teachers are still spiritual infants resounds with the thinking of Christian leaders in every generation. Hebrews 5 makes clear that the ongoing training of human discernment by the Scriptures brings a person to spiritual maturity.

ing point must be an overall philosophy of life that is thoroughly grounded in Scripture.

Priority also addresses the orientation of life. Although pleasure abounds in Scripture, God's commanding people to seek pleasure —to make entertainment a priority, or to set other things aside in favor of pleasure—seldom occurs. Moreover, all of the instances that *command* entertainment have additional significant theological purpose. These include the Sabbath rest and the feasts of Israel. While God made us capable of enjoying the pleasures that surround us, He did not make us to chase pleasure. Myers contends that the pursuing of pleasure communicates a false theology to the world. He advances that we live out "a culture of transcendence" that will turn the eyes of humanity to eternal values.[47]

We often fail to think about our entertainment choices. We simply assume that we are doing what is right without thoughtful and biblical evaluation. We choose arbitrarily instead of purposefully. Believers must differ from the pattern of their age. We must align our entertainment with God's priorities for our lives. We must observe broad patterns in Scripture and neglect nothing of worship and work. In a word, we must learn to rate leisure as God does. We can move toward this objective by asking, "What is the rightful place of entertainment in my life?" and then by answering that question on the basis of God's Word.

## Have a Godly Purposefulness in Activity

Although few commands in Scripture directly advocate purposeful activity, the tenor of God's Word contradicts the aimlessness or randomness of many humanistic philosophies.[48] The Westmin-

---

[47] *All God's Children*, xvi.

[48] This appears, for example, in the theme of God's sovereign purpose (Isa. 14:24–27; 19:12; 23:9; 46:11; Jer. 4:28; 26:3; Rom. 8:28; 9:11; Eph. 1:11; 3:11; 2 Tim. 1:9; 1 John

ster Shorter Catechism asks, "What is the chief end of man?" It answers, "Man's chief end is to glorify God, and to enjoy him for ever." Life has a purpose. God did not create senselessly. Even nature exists for divine purposes. Creation has the specific objective to glorify God at its core.[49]

> The heavens declare the glory of God; and the firmament sheweth his handywork. Day unto day uttereth speech, and night unto night sheweth knowledge. There is no speech nor language, where their voice is not heard. Their line is gone out through all the earth, and their words to the end of the world. (Ps. 19:1–4)

The believer ought to be able to identify a reason behind his actions. More specifically, he should bring glory to the Lord even through his entertainment choices. Myers goes so far as to claim, "The main question raised by popular culture concerns the most edifying way to spend one's time."[50] Why engage in this particular amusement? What value does it really have? Is there identifiable profit from this entertainment?[51]

In asking these questions, we do not have to give a profound theological answer every time or leave with a feeling of falsely induced guilt. Rest is just as much a biblical concept as work. Enjoying God by observing His creation and reveling in the pleasure that comes from His hand are righteous pursuits. These actions will not cause us to cower in the day of judgment. Yet there are also mind-

---

3:8). God determines the outcome of events and actions. He has a specific plan or objective toward which He propels all human history.

[49]The book of Revelation argues powerfully the summation of all things in and for Christ. He receives supreme exaltation alongside the Father (Rev. 5:1–3). See also Col. 1:15–18.

[50]*All God's Children*, 53.

[51]The entirety of O'Conner's *The Leisure Wasters* is devoted to exploring the failure to use leisure time in a constructive, purposeful manner. While the author does not write from a Christian perspective, she encourages a prudent use of time.

less, pointless acts of entertainment. As Myers observes, novelty and instant gratification do not serve as adequate life objectives.[52] Much modern entertainment drowns out the silence that allows us to think on eternity. We may watch television, play basketball, go fishing, play games with our children and reflect on the activity after the fact with disappointment or approval, depending on its accomplishment of legitimate purpose. Christians in particular must have an attitude of "redeeming the time" for Christ's sake (Eph. 5:16). We should evaluate our lives on the basis of purposefulness and use our allotted time carefully. Nevertheless, to parody Acts 15:10, if the apostles would not burden the Gentiles with the Mosaic Law, which was good and just, then it is not reasonable to create a legislated system of purposeful activity. A pattern of life that maintains a frenetic pace and demands investment of every moment while excluding pleasure and amusement has no scriptural warrant. God is glorified in our being the well-rounded creatures that He created us to be.

Realistically, we are much more prone to go to another extreme. Noting that God's Word does not absolutely command theologically purposeful activity in every case, we overlook the simpler verses that attach theological significance to all of life (e.g. 1 Cor. 10:31). Amusement must promote the glory of God. Though the specific reason for the entertainment may differ from person to person and case to case, in order to be righteous, our choices in entertainment must have a righteous purpose or goal.

This criterion for evaluating entertainment advocates at least some conscious thought concerning why we do a particular action. In responding to the question, "Why are you watching television?"

---

[52]Ibid., 64. He shows the implicit assumption in modern entertainment that "a new thing will be better than the old one," and he emphasizes the instability and vacuous quality of such reasoning.

we ought to be able to articulate a response consonant with Scripture. However, it would be a gross misapplication of the criterion to assume that every time we sit on our porch to enjoy the sunset we must first spend fifteen minutes contemplating the theological significance of a sunset. The principle of *purpose* reintroduces thoughtfulness, not bondage, to the believer. A better application of the principle might be a periodic consideration of the values of family vacation and an expression of those values to children who would otherwise see it as nothing more than another isolated event of life with no meaning. In those moments of reflection, we should not be at a loss to express purpose in his entertainment. If we *could not* respond with a scriptural answer to the question "Why?" then we ought to reconsider our actions very carefully; and we should always retain in our thoughts the fact that the ultimate cross-examiner of our answer is not man but God. This criterion causes us to ask, "What is the point, the value, or the purpose in my entertainment choice?"

## Exclude All That Defiles Purity

Few criteria for the evaluation of entertainment are as clear, or as clearly ignored, as the criterion of purity. *Holiness* occurs almost 600 times in Scripture. *Purity* adds another 100 instances, and *righteousness* adds almost 800. All three terms are absolutes. One act of ungodliness breaches holiness. A single impurity defiles purity. The slightest unrighteousness banishes righteousness. The issue of purity serves as probably the fiercest battleground in the entire debate over the Christian and entertainment. No one can deny the existence of the command for holiness. No one can refute the defiling quality of impurity. Haggai sets out a clear illustration of this in 2:11–14. Purity does not make impurity to be pure, but impurity pollutes purity. One pastor observed that "when you put on white gloves and play in the mud, you never make the mud glovey;

41

rather, you always makes the gloves muddy." A weak attempt at self-justification remains the only recourse. The defense of impurity in entertainment normally takes one of several basic tacks.

First, some people justify violence, immorality, and evil speech on the ground that it does not affect them. In addressing the issue of a person's "not being bothered" by the sin he sees in the movie, Wayne A. Wilson notes that the more important question to ask is, "*Should* this bother me? . . . A cold heart is not a reliable standard by which to live."[53] Though the visible effects of sin may arrive slowly, that slowness does not warrant a belief that no effect exists. The Bible warns against an attitude that associates the slow arrival of judgment with the absence of judgment (2 Pet. 3:3–4). Additionally, those who engage in this type of self-justification assume a position of omniscience. The pragmatist claims that he knows what *would* be true without participation in the entertainment, and he knows what *has* been due to his participation. He claims to know not only the present but the future. He knows not only the outcome but all potential outcomes. None of us has that kind of wisdom. Schultze observes, "Television teaches on many levels, not just through a show's overt message, and there is no way to determine precisely what one learns from the images and sounds emanating from the tube."[54] Even if we could know the outcome of an action, we still cannot justify what God has condemned. The Bible enjoins us to "follow . . . holiness, without which no man shall see the Lord" (Heb. 12:14), and "let no corrupt communication proceed out of your mouth, but that which is good to the use of edifying, that it may minister grace unto the hearers" (Eph. 4:29). The psalmist says of himself, "I will set no wicked thing

---

[53]*Worldly Amusements: Restoring the Lordship of Christ to Our Entertainment Choices* (Enumclaw, WA: WinePress Publishing, 1999), 92.

[54]*Redeeming Television*, 44.

before mine eyes: I hate the work of them that turn aside; it shall not cleave to me" (Ps. 101:3). The Scriptures everywhere exhort and demand separation from evil, not accommodation of it simply because we cannot perceive its effects.

Second, some people justify impurity on the ground that the Bible also depicts sin and evil. This betrays misunderstanding on several crucial points. It equates the power and effect of visual media with that of typographic media. This equation is neither biblically nor logically defensible. It is rationalization rather than reasoning. The fact that our culture demands visual stimuli contradicts this claim. People will not return to radio as their primary choice of entertainment because television imagery is much more captivating and powerful. Mankind possesses an immediate, intuitive awareness of the power of visual media that secular writers uniformly admit.[55] Words appeal to the mind. They require prior knowledge and maturity of experience for the reader to understand fully their import. For example, a person cannot fully grasp the meaning of Song of Solomon until he has reached a certain physical maturity and participatory awareness of God's plan for husbands and wives. Words communicate in linear and logical (or propositional) form. But visual media present material viscerally. Myers observes that one can evaluate the truth claim of writing but not of visual media. "An image cannot be true or false."[56] While a series of images may induce false thinking, imagery itself is not false. A movie could depict a criminal's successful bank heist and show no immediate consequences (inducing a person to believe that crime pays). The image itself is neither true nor false, but the implication may be. Hipps says, "The printed word is processed primarily in the left hemisphere of the brain, which specializes in logic, sequence,

---

[55]See Mander, *Four Arguments*, 43.
[56]*All God's Children*, 162.

and categories. In contrast, photographs and other imagery are processed primarily in the right hemisphere, which specializes in intuition and perceiving the *gestalt*—or everything at once."[57]

Scripture affirms the powerful intuitive effect that vision has on humanity. The New Testament gives hundreds of examples of sight and knowledge as the causes or grounds for an action.[58] Some forms of entertainment effectively remove knowledge from the equation and leave a person governed by an instinctive response to what he sees. In fact, television depends on this type of response. Commercials do not appeal to man's reason. They typically do not even address the qualities of a product. They seek to create a gut response to a product so that a person's feelings will override his reasoning processes at the store.[59] The programs that exist to retain the audience's attention until the next series of commercials follow the same procedure.

In addition, written words can communicate complex and abstract thought—both of which are virtually impossible for a visual medium. Few programs even attempt sustained logical thought; and those that make the effort usually fail. Visual media are precisely that—visual. Logic is not visible. One can make charts that depict logical thought, but rational and propositional thought are necessarily absent from visual media. Try to depict visually, for example,

---

[57] *The Hidden Power*, 75.

[58] The aorist participle from εἶδον ("I saw") occurs 108 times in the New Testament. Of these, at least 103 have a full causal or mild causal force with a result clearly specified in the context (see Acts 12:3 and 13:45 as representatives). Another three have concessive force (Matt. 21:32; John 20:29; 1 Pet. 1:8), maintaining the logical relationship between sight and action. Although sight does not rule an individual absolutely, it provides some of the most significant input in his decision-making process. Sight was one of the chief agents of Satan in encouraging Eve to sin (Gen. 3:6).

[59] These complaints come from within the industry. Coleen Cook, Malcolm Muggeridge, and Olga Martin have worked within the television industry itself for years. Neil Postman, William Romanowski, and Marvin Olasky have served as communications teachers and philosophers. All have written and critiqued their own industries extensively.

Christ's statement "Before Abraham was, I am." One could pan the camera out, show flashing stars (in the crude attempt to show the passing of time), show an old man in the desert, and a modern conjuring up of the presence of some divine light; but where is the propositional truth? It resides in language, not the image. God suits language uniquely for the communication of truth, and the attempt to use visual imagery in the place of language often distorts communication, not to mention reality. This same weakness appears clearly in the recent depiction of C. S. Lewis's *The Lion, the Witch, and the Wardrobe*. When the children hear the name of Aslan for the first time, the movie portrays them staring and smiling, but the viewer can infer any number of different motivations and sensations from their depiction. The book, however, makes clear exactly what the children experienced.[60] Each child sensed an entirely different thrill, but the movie could not communicate the difference. The visual image communicates viscerally but indistinctly. The typographic image communicates rationally and more clearly. This difficulty could be solved to some extent by a narrator's voice reading the story in the background of the movie, but such narration usually defeats the director's purposes.

In visual media each image replaces the preceding. Each requires immediate, full attention. The observer loses the trail of cause and effect.[61] This fact has severe consequences in distorting moral tone.[62] Even if a producer were to attempt an accurate portrayal of

---

[60] *The Lion, the Witch, and the Wardrobe* (1950; reprint, New York: Scholastic, 1995), 67–68.

[61] The complaint that a concentration on one medium (television) distorts the depiction of entertainment as a whole finds its answer in the observation that "television is thus not simply the dominant medium of *popular* culture, it is the single most significant shared reality in our entire society." Myers, *All God's Children*, 160.

[62] In describing the Hollywood Production Code of the 1930s, Olga J. Martin notes that "to satisfy the requirements for a moral thesis, the Code requirement must be satisfied which reads: 'Evil and good are never to be confused throughout the presenta-

David's adultery with Bathsheba, the visual moment would replace the logical and moral framework of the sin with a visceral one. The vast difference between a historical record of an action and the visual depiction of its occurrence becomes evident. In that instant the observer sees sin itself—not a *description* of sin, but a *depiction* of sin—in its alluring, enticing, physically interesting form. Someone had to sin in fact in order to depict the immorality on the screen. Flight, not perusal nor engagement, is the appropriate Christian response to immoral visual stimuli.[63]

> And when the woman saw that the tree was good for food, and that it was pleasant to the eyes, and a tree to be desired to make one wise, she took of the fruit thereof, and did eat, and gave also unto her husband with her; and he did eat. (Gen. 3:6)

> I will set no wicked thing before mine eyes: I hate the work of them that turn aside; it shall not cleave to me. (Ps. 101:3)

> And if thine eye offend thee, pluck it out: it is better for thee to enter into the kingdom of God with one eye, than having two eyes to be cast into hell fire. (Mark 9:47)[64]

Even more importantly, those who equate Hollywood's depiction of sin (even in those instances where it treats sin negatively) and the Bible's depiction of sin are forgetting a crucial facet of theology —bibliology. The Bible is God's Word; Hollywood is not. This

---

tion.'" *Hollywood's Movie Commandments* (New York: Arno Press, 1970), 102. Yet this exact moral confusion prevails in modern mass-media industries.

[63]In this realm Romanowski errs philosophically. When he omits the sinful quality of the portrayal itself from consideration, his noble and righteous desire to see all things brought under the power of Christ swerves aside to permit or solicit sin. *Eyes Wide Open*, 84–87.

[64]See also the pointed observations on immorality in Prov. 7:6–23. The young man who remains in the place of temptation is practicing not wisdom but moral folly. 2 Timothy 2:22 encourages flight from youthful lusts, not indulgence in them.

should not be a difficult concept to grasp, but many believers obscure the distinction. We ought not think, even for a moment, that a God Who knows the exact boundary between good and evil, knows perfectly the nature of man, and knows how to communicate truth perfectly should be required to justify Himself beside an industry created for financial profit, dedicated to popular art, and permeated with philosophical humanism. The argument that justifies impurity in entertainment on the basis of the Bible's depiction of sin crosses the line into outright blasphemy. God never seduces anyone to evil (James 1:13). Hollywood regularly does. God *is* truth, *is* light, and *is* love. It could be argued that Hollywood knows little of the true meaning of these things. In its fallen condition humanity is rarely capable of touching on moral issues with the forthright delicacy, the perfect moral rectitude, the holy zeal, and the just depiction of consequence that the Bible evidences. Instead of drawing a person into sin, the Bible sends him fleeing from it. Such cannot be said for even the noblest intentions of the television industry.[65]

Third, some will justify impure themes as artistic amusement. Muggeridge notes the irony that the BBC has inscribed the following at the entrance to its Broadcasting House:

> This temple of the arts and muses is dedicated to Almighty God by the first governors of broadcasting in the year 1931, Sir John Reith being Governor General. It is their prayer that good seeds sown may bring forth a good harvest, that all things hostile to peace or purity may be banished from this house, that the people, inclining their ears to whatso-

---

[65]For a thorough discussion of the proper presentation of objectionable elements in Scripture, see "Christian Educational Censorship" in Ronald A. Horton, ed., *Christian Education: Its Mandate and Mission* (Greenville, SC: Bob Jones University Press, 1992), 45–70. The article is also available online at http://www.bjupress.com/resources/articles/objectionable_elements.html.

ever things are beautiful, honest, and of good report, may tread the paths of wisdom and righteousness.[66]

The BBC now supports all manner of depravity under the guise of art. It claims that a tasteful or artistic depiction of anything natural to humanity is beneficial. Scripture addresses this argument in a more indirect than direct fashion. It castigates the delight in the exposure of others (Hab. 2:15).[67] It demonstrates that the *natural* thing may be immoral (1 Cor. 6:13). It warns strongly against engaging in an activity that could cause oneself or another believer to sin (Matt. 18:6). And it represents visual imagery as particularly seductive in its attraction of the heart (Gen. 3:6; Exod. 20:4). While it is true that nakedness was once the natural and undefiled state of humanity, the fall brought limitations to even this natural state. What once brought no shame should now produce great shame outside of the context of marriage. What once could not incite sin may now generate profound evil. Robert DeMoss Jr. observes rightly, "When it comes to developing a world-life view, especially as it pertains to the arena of the arts and entertainment, it is our view of God that is the heart of the matter. The smaller my view of God, His power and His majesty, the more likely I am to tolerate, yes, even enjoy art that is morally offensive to Him."[68]

Finally, a person could respond to impurity in entertainment in a manner that delights in sin and does not even attempt to justify it. This is the current state of Hollywood, television, and the pop music industry.[69] "In one survey, three-fourths of single Christian

---

[66]*Christ and the Media*, 25.

[67]It is possible that Ham's sin in Gen. 9:20–25 involved his being amused and entertained by the nakedness of his father.

[68]*TV: The Great Escape*, 114.

[69]Michael Medved documents the assault on morality in *Hollywood vs. America* (New York: HarperCollins, 1992). The extent of depravity in popular culture can hardly be understated. "[Television] is a medium that refers to sex outside of marriage *thirteen times* more frequently than it mentions intimacy between husband and wife" (117). The

adults thought 'movies containing vulgarities, explicit sex, nudity, and antibiblical messages had an adverse effect on their moral and spiritual condition,' but at least half of these same people approved of films that included these very ingredients."[70] "A 1991 Gallup Poll showed that 58 percent of the American public said they are offended frequently or occasionally by current television programming," but we refuse to turn off the trash.[71] Sometimes we simply forget God's Word when we are engaged in entertainment. Scripture applies, in our minds, to grand theological realms but not to daily living. We can be guilty of forming a radical disconnection between God's Word and life. If we persist in viewing impure themes, we will eventually dull our spiritual senses. Scripture specifically attests that the abundance of sin in a culture can breed coldness in the hearts of God's people (Matt. 24:12). Lot and his family experienced this apathy. The Bible records that his soul was grieved by sin (2 Pet. 2:7–8), but Genesis also shows his unwillingness to give up the pleasures of Sodom (Gen. 19:16). His wife grew so accustomed to Sodom that she turned back and lost her life (Gen. 19:26).

Christians do not consciously desire to leave a life's record of apathy toward sin, but entertainment can erode the spiritual instinct and dull the conscience when a person becomes a lover of pleasure. (Contrast 2 Tim. 3:4 with Heb. 11:25.) The self-centered, pleasure-loving mindset reflects the fallen condition of humanity (Titus 3:3), but it does not reflect Christ. Consequently we must evaluate our entertainment choices against the standard of purity and ask, "Are my entertainment choices holy?"

---

double-entendre is relentless (118), the attack on marriage, profound. "Hollywood may be the only community in the world in which the assumption that a long-term couple might actually be married could be construed as some sort of insult" (140).

[70]Romanowski, *Eyes Wide Open*, 30. This fact combines the criteria of purity and domination into a symbiotic relationship. Christians allow themselves to fall under the dominion of pleasure to such an extent that they disregard holiness.

[71]Medved, 118.

## Build Edifying Relationships

Entertainment intersects humanity on the foundational level of relationships. Some pleasures serve a constructive purpose: they build others emotionally, spiritually, physically, or socially. This serves as additional evidence that entertainment, *per se*, is not evil. A parent may wrestle with his children, play basketball, go fishing, and play other games with them in a constructive fashion. By righteous interaction he molds character, strength, and skill in them. People of all ages compete in races, attend picnics, splash in the ocean, and watch sunsets together. Thousands of amusements offer profitable interaction in edifying ways. In justifying his own choices of pleasure, the apostle Paul specifically addressed this issue (1 Cor. 10:23). Entertainment should not deconstruct humanity. When it builds others, it is valuable. When it cuts down (Eph. 4:29) or isolates people from each other, it contradicts the expressed purposes of God. For example, Hipps believes that "electronic culture has turned us into a tribe of individuals."[72] We are being torn apart by our amusements. Some of our favorite entertainments, especially when taken to an extreme, destroy meaningful relationships with those around us. Paul Borgman notes, "Like the Pied Piper, television is able to lure. And like the Pied Piper, TV seems to lead its young audience right out of their parents' lives. Families seem to drift apart. Children disappear not only from family life but from the town and even the world of their parents."[73] His solution is not a reactionary dismissal of television; instead he encourages parents to guide the family's use of TV toward constructive goals.

When we use entertainment improperly, it can lead to the breaking down of relationships. We act paradoxically as a unit (in that we share the same values), but the values that we share separate us

---

[72] *The Hidden Power*, 105.
[73] *TV*, 21.

from each other (unbridled selfishness, personal freedom, tolerance). Some forms of entertainment do great harm to the fellowship of believers and to constructive society. If entertainment breaks down husband-wife, parent-child, neighbor-neighbor relationships rather than cementing them through edification, that entertainment runs contrary to Scripture. Modern entertainment culture often overemphasizes our individualism. By doing so, it contradicts God's Word.

For example, when Leviticus 19:18 commissions us, "Thou shalt love thy neighbour as thyself: I am the Lord," it requires our making deliberate choices for the good of others. It is extremely difficult to show love toward your neighbor when you hole up in a room by yourself for hours in self-amusement.

First Corinthians 12:25–26 urges, "For as the body is one, and hath many members, and all the members of that one body, being many, are one body: so also is Christ. . . . That there should be no schism in the body; but that the members should have the same care one for another. And whether one member suffer, all the members suffer with it; or one member be honoured, all the members rejoice with it." This type of interaction and mutual care of members cannot occur when the members are totally disconnected. If our entertainments become narcissistic, they fail the scriptural test of edification. If the parable of the good Samaritan were told today, the Levite and priest could easily be replaced by the couch potato and video gamer who have no time to help others since they are so busy with the important pursuits of self-enjoyment.

> And by chance there came down a certain priest that way: and when he saw him, he passed by on the other side. And likewise a Levite, when he was at the place, came and looked on him, and passed by on the other side. But a certain Samaritan, as he journeyed, came where he was: and when he saw him, he had compassion on him. (Luke 10:25–37)

The rise of an entire class of entertainments known collectively as "extreme fighting" illustrates the destructive potential of amusement gone awry. In imitation of ancient gladiatorial contests, these fights specialize in brutalizing an opponent in a savage display of power. Christians of the early church condemned and eventually outlawed this type of brutal spectacle. They recognized that the deliberate maltreatment of other human beings for pleasure expresses depravity, not holiness. God calls his people to constructive relationships and the exhibition of love. He does not encourage the exhibition of misery. Other examples of this mistreatment of humanity occur in the deliberate humiliations, deprivations, and miseries caused by various reality television series. Scripture never permits our preying upon the wretchedness of others for personal enjoyment.

Television represents a class of amusement that often disintegrates relationships rather than builds them. In one sense it unites people —hundreds of millions of people can watch the same program at the same time—but it also isolates them.[74] Instead of talking with each other, interacting, even playing, they stare at a screen. DeMoss pushes the argument to its natural conclusion: "With TV around we live together—all alone. Call it mutual isolation. We're collectively separate. . . . Even if everything presented on television were wholesome, uplifting, instructive, and pro-social, for the most part the act of watching TV divides people from each other."[75] Yet few programs could be considered truly constructive

---

[74]Gunther Anders argues this point forcefully. He sees a truncating of human relationships in the solo quality of television performance, in the breakup of family communication, in the destruction of the ability to communicate well with each other, in the selfish consumptive nature of the entertainment, in the absence of personal experience of the world, and in the debasing effect of low-culture presentations that govern the radio and television industries. Even secularists show concern for the influence of amusement on culture, especially the ability to relate to other people. "The Phantom World of TV," in *Mass Culture: The Popular Arts in America*, ed. Bernard Rosenberg and David Manning White (Glencoe, IL: Free Press, 1957), 358–67.

[75]*TV*, 33.

and "wholesome." Obviously, when the abysmal social record of some entertainments is included in this analysis, the case becomes even stronger. Television mocks adults, depicts teens as the most intelligent and wise members of society, ridicules the family (especially one with a loving relationship between one husband and one wife for life), and emphasizes social tensions (including hatred, violence, bitterness, anger, and frustration). The glorification of individualism and self-reliance seen in most programs contradicts a balanced sense of community and dependence on God. As believers we recognize that the standard of Scripture is determinative in the realm of relationships. When Paul admonishes the people of God to "follow after the things which make for peace, and things wherewith one may edify another" (Rom. 14:19), he reveals the mind of God for the believer. When believers receive the injunctions to "walk in love" (Eph. 5:2) and to "keep the unity of the Spirit" (Eph. 4:3), they must recognize their responsibility to interact in a righteous manner socially. The Christian needs to examine his entertainment in light of God's standards and reject that which damages right relationships. We should ask ourselves, "Is there any harm or good being done to others in my use of entertainment?"

## Exhibit Discerning Wisdom and Hold Fast to Truth

Many people want to suspend critical thinking when being entertained. To them the entertainment exists to provide relaxation from all thought and action.[76] This attitude produces a tremendous potential for moral failure on the part of the believer. The suspension of critical thinking, a crucial aspect of biblical wisdom

---

[76]Myers defends the need for careful thought: "Saying that wisdom calls us to think is hardly a denial of God's authority, or to suggest that God is indifferent about what decisions we make. Pascal once said that the first of all moral obligations is to think clearly, and the Proverbs are quite emphatic that obedience to God requires 'a disciplined and prudent life' (Proverbs 1:3), which must surely involve clear thinking." *All God's Children*, 35.

and discernment, leads to a careless imbibing of whatever poisons occur in a particular entertainment. We must engage in concerted effort to avoid falling prey to sin. Wisdom, as depicted in Proverbs, is acutely aware of its surroundings. It refuses to suspend critical thinking for even a moment. The simpleton and the naïve suffer ruin by their lack of wisdom. Those who refuse to maintain the alertness of wisdom find themselves caught in various snares, including immorality (Prov. 7:7–23), inappropriate speech (Prov. 18:7, 20:25), and anger (Prov. 22:25).

In addition, some forms of entertainment may weaken our capacity to reason.[77] Shane Hipps observes, "The rise of image-based communication in our culture weakened our preference for abstract and linear thought patterns in favor of more concrete, holistic, and nonlinear approaches to the world."[78] Although the brain is not totally impoverished by passive entertainment, it can experience a sensory deprivation that weakens our ability to think correctly about what we observe.[79]

Some writers claim that due to its visceral appeal visual entertainment may weaken the ability to perceive abstract truth accurately. Neil Postman notes that the second commandment

---

[77]Shane Hipps draws heavily on the writings of Marshall McLuhan in critiquing the medium of television in its entirety. "We are oblivious to the ways the medium, regardless of its content, reduces our capacity for abstract thought, makes us prefer intuition and experience over logic and reasoning, and revives tribal experiences in an individualistic culture." *The Hidden Power*, 38. "As our thinking patterns begin to mirror this communication pattern [of TV], we find it only natural to deny any sense of a *metanarrative*, an overarching story or truth that organizes and makes sense of all other truths" (68). "The glut of disparate, often contradictory, and random data with no center or margin has begun to erode our belief in a metanarrative" (68).

[78]Ibid., 72. As a proponent of the emerging church, Hipps argues in favor of a jettisoning of traditional propositional doctrine in favor of a "conversation" on truth.

[79]Mander reacts strongly to this diminution of human reason. *Four Arguments*, 157–69.

is a strange injunction to include as part of an ethical system *unless its author assumed a connection between forms of human communication and the quality of a culture.* We may hazard a guess that a people who are being asked to embrace an abstract, universal deity would be rendered unfit to do so by the habit of drawing pictures or making statues or depicting their ideas in any concrete, iconographic forms. The God of the Jews was to exist in the Word and through the Word, an unprecedented conception requiring the highest order of abstract thinking.[80]

Postman seems to miss the point. The images addressed in the second commandment are images used in representing *God* in worship. We know this because pictures appeared in other aspects of tabernacle worship. For example, pomegranates and bells adorned the robes of the high priest (Exod. 28), and cherubim adorned the curtains of the tabernacle (Exod. 26:1). God prohibited the use of any image representing Himself because the image tends to supplant Him (the image seems to be more *real* simply because it is *visible*). In addition images are unable to depict His essence and character fully and accurately, since He is spirit (John 4:24). It would be wrong to conclude from this instruction on proper worship that all art or visual entertainment weakens the mind and spirit. It would be better for us to affirm that an overuse of images to the neglect of propositional truth weakens the ability to reason abstractly.

Society does not use entertainment in a balanced fashion, though. It pursues leisure with religious devotion. It does neglect careful reasoning in favor of the holistic impressions gleaned from imagery. The regular devoting of ourselves to mind-weakening amusements is a capitulation of wisdom to folly. Anything that diminishes the

---

[80] *Amusing Ourselves,* 9.

capacity to discern right from wrong, to comprehend spiritual truth, and to act decisively upon that truth is a threat to spiritual life. In a culture that worships entertainment, God cannot receive worship unless He is supremely entertaining.[81] Through wisdom we refuse to be lulled into weak thinking.

Wisdom rightly appraises the consequences of an action. It foresees the evil that lies along certain paths of life and avoids those paths (Prov. 27:12). It examines not only the immediate content of entertainment (whether violence, immorality, blasphemy, deception, hedonism, or any other thing contrary to sound doctrine occurs) but the effect of entertainment as well. T. M. Moore wonders at the inability of the natural mind to perceive the simplest cause-and-effect relationships between entertainment and cultural life.[82] Yet few of us have thoroughly considered the long-term consequences of our amusements. With Scripture's repeated emphasis on the need for proper discernment, it almost goes without saying that the criterion of wisdom would be applicable to entertainment. We should rightly ask whether a particular form of entertainment is promoting wisdom or folly—whether it is debasing man's ability to think and discern correctly or is heightening his biblical and natural awareness of reality.

In practicing right discernment, the believer must guard the truth. Mass entertainment in particular communicates the philosophy, values, and worldview of its producers.[83] By necessity it conveys the

---

[81]See T. S. Eliot's defining of the inextricable link between culture and religion in "Notes Towards the Definition of Culture" in *Christianity and Culture* (New York: Harcourt Brace Jovanovich, 1968), 100. A culture that excludes God as nonexistent, unnecessary, or irrelevant reflects that opinion in its amusements.

[82]*Redeeming Pop Culture*, 3.

[83]Romanowski, *Eyes Wide Open*, 97. Romanowski encourages a highly interactive approach to world culture. Some of his examples that see biblical philosophy in popular culture are stretched. The absorbing of unbiblical philosophy in hundreds of aspects of popular culture in the attempt to find some redeeming value does not resonate

attitudes of its writers and directors toward good and evil. When those attitudes contradict Scripture, we must consciously reject them. The Christian parent must also consider his children's exposure to and consumption of worldly philosophy. Without a mature biblical framework of good and evil, children are even more prone to believe and to imitate what they see. Parents must guard against a lifestyle that allows children to hear and incorporate falsehood into their lives throughout the week while setting truth before them briefly on Sundays. The Christian parent has the obligation to defend the truth before his children, not just hold it quietly to himself.

## Summary

All of these criteria stem from Scripture and respond to its Author. When taken together, these criteria provide each of us with a standard for evaluating his amusements. We cannot elect to have no standard. Entertainment insists on evaluation by its very nature.[84] We may make our choices based on momentary pleasure or eternal truth, but we cannot escape the fact that some motive underlies our selection.

---

with biblical wisdom. Moreover, his justifying a visual depiction of depravity in order to communicate truly about culture overlooks crucial differences between visual and typographical media. Television differs from print media in making every viewer an eyewitness of the event. For example, he writes, *"Dead Man Walking . . .* contains horrific scenes of violence and rape that, while difficult to watch, reveal the depth of evil that has taken place." Ibid., 102. The believer does not have to view sin itself in order to sense the horror involved. His sense of horror is defined by God's Word. However, Romanowski evaluates accurately the unbiblical philosophy conveyed in the melodrama of television. He utterly rejects its utopian and humanistic depiction of the goodness of man, and he observes that those who are concerned with truth must depict people as they truly are—sinful yet doing some good things—and the world as it truly is. Ibid., 108–20. Romanowski addresses primarily how a Christian participant in popular culture (as an actor, director, writer, composer) should reflect biblical truth.

[84]Romanowski provides a "matrix" through which the believer can run a specific cultural element. He suggests some penetrating questions that promote a biblical evaluation of all human culture. *Eyes Wide Open*, 155–61.

# 3

# A BIBLICAL GUIDE TO ENTERTAINMENT

## THE SOURCES OF ENTERTAINMENT

Entertainment has two sources. The first is its ultimate source, and the other is an indirect source. The ultimate source of entertainment (not to say of every individual form of entertainment) is God. As argued below, Scripture presents Him as the Creator of all good pleasure. The indirect source of entertainment is leisure time. Entertainment is limited when people have little leisure time. Many writers marvel at the phenomenon of modern leisure. In many previous generations humanity struggled to survive. In fact, this struggle still appears in the less industrialized nations. Work circumscribed entertainment. Daylight limited its duration. The technological advances of the twentieth century opened a cultural chasm between pre-industrial and industrial societies.[1] People now expect to devote a significant portion of each day, week, and year to entertainment. The ecstatic state of pleasure-worship that has resulted is philosophically troubling to the believer, who recognizes that unchecked frivolity erodes both a sense of divine purpose and an awareness of eternity. Yet few wish for a return to pre-industrial society. Electricity, motors, and mechanical devices have created greater diversification of occupation, greater mobility, and greater leisure. Apart from catastrophic societal upheaval, significant discretionary time is likely to remain a dominant feature of culture. Modern society raises serious questions for the believer,

---

[1]See Nels Anderson, *Work and Leisure* (New York: Free Press of Glencoe, 1961), 1–24.

and the Christian's worldview forces him to answer the question "How shall I use rightly my leisure time?" Entertainment serves as one possible answer.

## A BIBLICAL PHILOSOPHY OF HUMANITY

Entertainment exists universally in human culture. The forms differ widely, but the fact of entertainment is uniform.[2] "Everyone plays; the need to do something for relaxation is built into the biology and psychology of human beings."[3] The written testimony of Scripture combined with archaeological records of ancient Palestine provide important information on entertainments in Israel. Both attest a less commercially oriented entertainment style than that of many surrounding nations; however, amusement did exist. William Taylor Smith comments, "Games evidently took a less prominent place in Heb life than in that of the Greeks, the Romans and the Egyptians. Still the need for recreation was felt and to a certain extent supplied in ways according with the national temperament. Mere athletics (apart from Gr and Rom influence) were but little cultivated. Simple and natural amusements and exercises and trials of wit and wisdom, were more to the Heb taste."[4] Neither Israel nor its neighbors were at all familiar with mass-media entertainment on the scale that humanity experiences today.

---

[2]See Marguerite Ickis, *The Book of Games and Entertainment the World Over* (New York: Dodd, Mead, 1969). She cites scores of games from nations in all parts of the globe. In addition, a diachronological study of entertainment shows that though the accepted forms differ from age to age, the use of entertainment is pervasive in all times and cultures. See, for example, Nash, *Recreation*, 13–42; M. J. Ellis, *Why People Play* (Englewood Cliffs, NJ: Prentice-Hall, Inc., 1973); Caillois, *Man, Play and Games*; and Neumeyer and Neumeyer, *Leisure and Recreation*.

[3]Daniels, xi.

[4]"Games," *The International Standard Bible Encyclopaedia*, ed. James Orr (Grand Rapids: Eerdmans, 1956), 2:1168–73. See concurring testimony on the difference between Babylonian and Israeli recreation in Kraus, 134–35.

However, both participated heavily in public entertainment of a non-commercial type.[5]

The universal occurrence of amusement in human culture leads to several possible conclusions. Either entertainment is a product of the Fall and, thereby, transferred its effect to all sinful humanity, or it is a natural part of created humanity. These are the only options that explain the scope of what we observe. The Scriptures exclude the first option. If amusement were entirely or exclusively evil—a part of fallen, sinful humanity—the Bible could not fail to address it as such. Entertainment should receive special condemnation alongside other sins. Not only is such condemnation lacking, but many passages imply the opposite—that entertainment, used within God-ordained parameters, is good.[6] The second option must be true. Entertainment is part of naturally created humanity. This raises two additional possibilities. Entertainment either adheres to something in God's own essence (and man was made in God's image), or it pertains to something in human creatureliness. The better answer seems to be the former one,[7] though certain forms of entertainment may stem from our being creatures.

Our desire to experience amusement, delight, or pleasure answers to the delight and pleasure that God takes in His biblically defined "rest." That God delights in His creation the Bible makes clear. True, His pleasure and interest compare only loosely with the pleasure and interest that humanity experiences due to our difference in being, but that cannot minimize the fact that God worked in the creation (Gen. 1), rested from His work (Gen. 2), and now takes pleasure in observing and interacting with His creation. The repetition of טוֹב ("good") throughout Genesis 1 makes

---

[5]Ibid.

[6]See the section below entitled "The Biblical Data Concerning Entertainment."

[7]See the section below entitled "The Admission of Pleasure in the Divine Character."

clear that God delighted in the result of His creative activity. Since we are sub-creators, we take His delight, amusement, and pleasure from work for which we are only partly responsible. We can be entertained by God's work, our own work, or the work of others. This defense of entertainment does not equate modern popular entertainment with anything residing in the character of God, but it does claim that the capacity for and the will to experience interest and amusement apart from work has some connection with the character of God. From Scripture we know that the image of God in man was severely marred in the Fall, but it was not destroyed. Likewise, our proper use of entertainment is marred. It is now subject to serious abuses, but it has not been repealed or destroyed.[8]

If this depiction of the theological underpinning for human activity is accurate, we should think carefully about our position as image-bearers.[9] We seldom take the time to consider our humanity as defined by the Scriptures. Even systematic theology texts rarely explore the full scope of God-intended qualities of humanity. Instead they usually touch on man's abilities and natural tendencies only briefly before they rush on to explain his constitution and his sin.[10]

---

[8]See Millard J. Erickson, *Christian Theology* (Grand Rapids: Baker, 1985), 513. Reformed theologians generally distinguish between the essential and accidental image of God in humanity and would place pleasure in the accidental. Charles Hodge, *Systematic Theology*, (Reprint, Grand Rapids: Eerdmans, 1997), 2:98–99; Robert L. Dabney, *Systematic Theology*, 2nd ed. (1878; reprint, Avon: The Bath Press, 1996), 293–96.

[9]People assume that their own definitions of good and evil are correct. Believers must derive their understanding from Scripture in the first place rather than look for justification afterwards. Daniels observes this defect in Puritan standards for entertainment: "By and large Puritans evaluated the goodness and badness of sports and games by historical and empirical criteria, not by scriptural or theological argument." *Puritans at Play*, 183.

[10]A survey of major works of systematic theology shows that the most common topics include man's origin, the "image of God," the natural composition of man (including the dichotomist and trichotomist debate), and man's sin nature. The researcher must look to books on ethics, culture, and Christian anthropology as well as to individual commentaries in order to provide a thorough view of man. See, for example, Meredith Kline, *Kingdom Prologue* (published privately, 1986), 1:55–59, cited in Myers, *All God's*

A failure to study the full breadth of humanity as created by God yields a truncated perspective. The student learns to define an individual as a spiritual/physical being, but he does not learn to explore deeply the parameters of genuine humanity. When we work, write, build, imagine, and play, are we expressing something inherent or auxiliary to humanity? Were we created exclusively for work and worship? A careful examination of the biblical statements on the natural condition of humanity aids in the construction of a biblical philosophy of man. A more accurate and ordered philosophy of man leads to a more biblical philosophy of entertainment.[11]

## The Nature of Humanity in the Created Order

Three qualities that have bearing on our use of entertainment stand out in comparing people to the animals in the creation. First, while we are creatures, humans are distinct from all other creatures. We share some traits with animals, but our essence is also radically different. Genesis 1:26 tells us that man was made in the image of God. This special status sets us apart from the rest of creation.[12] This image means, in part, that we possess a spiritual existence that will never end. Like the animals we require rest, food, drink, and interaction with other members of our species. Unlike the animals, however, our current actions have ramifications for eternity. Like the animals we enjoy frolicking, cavorting, playing all manner

---

*Children*, 39–40, 44. Myers addresses the broader scope of popular culture, but many of the analyses and criticisms apply equally to the narrower topic of entertainment. Entertainment has become largely a subset of popular culture, and popular culture is decidedly entertainment-oriented. Myers's work has the additional value of thorough research and citation of both religious and secular authors who recognize the deficiencies of American entertainment.

[11]Erickson notes, "Extraordinary care must be taken to formulate correctly our understanding of man. The conclusions reached here will affect, if not determine, our conclusions in other areas of doctrine." *Christian Theology*, 457.

[12]See Hodge, *Systematic Theology*, 2:96–99, for a detailed look at what this image is and implies.

of games. Unlike the animals, our choice of sport and enjoyment has enduring consequences.

Second, God created us with intellectual and moral choice. Instead of naming the animals on His own, God brought them to Adam and entrusted their naming to him. The first man served as a sub-creator under God in relation to those things under his dominion. His choice of each animal's name did not necessarily have deep theological motivation or import in reference to the animal, but it did reflect something significant about humanity. God created humanity with discretion and imagination, and He called these capacities good. We still possess this capacity to create under God's authority. As long as we do not violate God's command, our choices in architecture, art, music, entertainment, and all the other facets of life reflect the beautiful diversity that God has ordained. That diversity brings Him glory as long as it is used in submission to Him. We can survey a barren stretch of land and envision a beautiful colonnade of marble, a trellis of cascading roses, or a tranquil pond. We can hear the sweet strands of lilting music, the bombast of a mighty band, or the complex harmonies of symphony without the presence of a single instrument. In fact, it is well established that Beethoven wrote his Ninth Symphony and his final six string quartets and piano sonatas after he had gone completely deaf. We can bring about much of what we imagine, and we imagine diversely. Legitimate diversity reflects powerfully the glory and dominion of the Creator.

We create in imitation of God, but our creation must concur with the moral character of the great Creator. Adam experienced free moral choice in the garden of Eden. When he fell, his disobedience to God's commands did not rescind his capacity to reason. Further, the Fall did not take away our ability to choose. It marred our imaginations and warped our will to use our time wisely and righteously, but it did not revoke discretionary activity altogether. This means that our entertainments reflect something of the creativity and freedom to choose that God ordained to be part of humanity.

Third, many aspects of creation reflect God's desire to bring pleasure to mankind. Pleasure is not always possible in a fallen creation, but the original created order was thoroughly pleasing. In the creation, pleasure included the stimulating of man's sight, taste, and health in the creation of trees good for food (Gen. 2:9), the stimulating of man's activity in both cultivation and metallurgical activity (Gen. 2:10–12), the stimulation of his mind in naming the animals (Gen. 2:19–20), and the stimulating of his social interaction, spiritual nature, and sexual nature in the creation of woman (Gen. 2:16–25).

All of these pleasurable experiences are, in some sense, unnecessary to life. They are gratuitous. They are almost frivolous or excessive in their sensory stimulation. God could have created one bland option for man's food. He could have made the earth drab in color, sound, and texture. He could have left Adam without social interaction. And even if He desired to create a woman, He could have constructed human interaction exclusively on the spiritual rather than the physical and social planes. In God's creation, pleasure was not an afterthought; it was forethought. Diversity and enjoyment are intentional, not incidental or accidental. The natural state as created by God is fully good. The claim that man's ultimate pleasure is mutually exclusive to God's will derives from Satan, not from Scripture. Satan was the first to question the goodness of God. In the garden he argued that either Eve or God could be pleased, but not both. He depicted man's enjoyment and God's will as opposites, but his depiction was fraudulent. From the beginning, God created people to rejoice in everything good, to delight in all the diversity that comes from His hand, and to take pleasure in things small and great.

In C. S. Lewis's *The Screwtape Letters*, the old devil Screwtape observes to his nephew, Wormwood, "Never forget that when we are dealing with any pleasure in its healthy and normal and satisfying form, we are, in a sense, on the Enemy's ground. I know we have won many a soul through pleasure. All the same, it is His invention, not ours. He made the pleasures: all our research so far has not enabled us to produce one. All we can do is to encourage the humans to take the pleasures which our Enemy has produced, at times, or in ways, or in degrees, which He has forbidden."[13]

In the original creation, mankind rejoiced in the fruit of his own labor and the labor of others. The viewpoint that insists a person may delight only in his own labor—claiming that he has no right to be entertained by the arts and activities of others—tacitly rejects man's appreciation for the work of God. If we cannot take pleasure from observing the work of others, then we cannot take pleasure in observing the work of God. Such thinking does not reflect the Scriptures rightly. The psalms, for example, are full of joyful reflection on the works of the Lord. (See Ps. 77:11–20 as a clear example.) On the other hand, if we ascribe such value to the work of other people that we forget that their activity is sub-creative, we may cross a theological line into humanism. Entertainment should take pleasure from our own work or the work of others, but it must receive that pleasure in a proper manner, recognizing that God's power and goodness are the ultimate source.

That people had at least the time for leisure in this created state derives logically from the opening chapters of Genesis. The curse brought hardship in work to humanity (Gen. 3:17–19). The Fall required

---

[13](West Chicago: Lord & King Associates, 1976), 54.

him to expend greater resources of time and energy just to survive. If we have time for entertainment in a fallen world where the earth resists subjection to our hands, Adam must have had even greater time when the earth yielded gladly to his dominion. Frustration comes when we labor but have no time or capacity to enjoy the fruit of labor. We work but cannot rest from and delight in our work. We refer to this as the "rat race," but something in our hearts yearns for times of rest from and enjoyment in our labor. In the future rescinding of the curse, God promises to bring a physical condition to the earth in which we can revel in the end state of our labor (Isa. 65:21–23). We now labor to survive. Adam once labored to enjoy. The appreciation of the product of labor, then, is a perfectly good and natural state of humanity. We should conclude that the nature of man in the created order permitted and encouraged him to experience appropriate pleasure.

## The Pleasure of Mankind in the Divine Plan

The remainder of the Bible will bear out the preceding argument in its references to feasting, singing, dancing, and playing. "Feasting, songs, music, and especially dancing, were the commonest form of relaxation. Opportunity was taken for this at every domestic rejoicing (Jer. 31:4), including merry-making at harvest (Judg. 9:27; 21:21) as well as at such public and state functions as the royal accession (1 Kings 1:40) or celebration of victory (Exod. 15:20; Judg. 11:34; 1 Sam. 18:6). Story-telling and the art of propounding riddles was also a highly-esteemed practice (Judg. 14:12; Ezek. 17:2; 1 Kings 10:1)."[14] God appointed three major feasts in the life of the nation of Israel. True, the feasts had supreme spiritual purpose and significance, but God chose times of joy and pleasure to reflect important truths about Himself. "Religious commitment

---

[14]D. J. Wiseman, "Games," *New Bible Dictionary*, 3rd ed., ed. J. D. Douglas (Downers Grove, IL: InterVarsity, 1996), 396.

was not incompatible with pleasure in temporal things conceived as gifts of God."[15] God's deliverance of His people physically and spiritually produces joy, not stoicism (Feast of Unleavened Bread). His gifts bring vitality and security rather than dearth and fear (Feast of Weeks). His abiding presence with His people is cause for pleasure, not anguish (Feast of Tabernacles). In each of these required feasts, the people of Israel stopped all unnecessary labor for a week's time, joined in a collective body, and reveled in the goodness of God. Food, drink, music, and social interaction commingled in producing times of delightful, entertaining rest.[16]

Scripture also indicates that God will restore singing, dancing, and playing to His people in the future. Biblical descriptions of the final restoration of Israel include singing over vineyards (Isa. 27:2; Hosea 2:15), shouting in joy over the blooming of the desert (Isa. 35:1–2, 6), and singing of the hills (Isa. 55:12). Even though the imagery is figurative, the point remains intact: God causes His people to delight in and be pleased by the things He has made for them. Similarly, the depictions of the millennial kingdom paint an image of genuine delight and pleasure. We find a marriage feast (Matt. 25:1–13; Rev. 19:9), a newly created heaven and earth (Rev. 21:1), a beautifully adorned city (Rev. 21:2, 11–21), the complete absence of anything that causes pain or sorrow (Rev. 21:4), and an abundance of perfect food and drink (Rev. 22:1–3, 17).

Although some of this imagery could represent a guarantee of eternal provision, much of it directly addresses pleasure. The imagery of the marriage feast in particular expresses the righteous potential for entertainment. Wedding feasts offer amusement, cessation of

---

[15]D. Freeman, "Feasts," *New Bible Dictionary*, 365.

[16]See the chapter on leisure in Ralph Gower, *The New Manners and Customs of Bible Times* (Chicago: Moody Press, 1987), 301–16, for a documentation of the entertainment activities common in Bible times.

labor, and deliberate experiencing of pleasure. They provide entertainment *par excellence*. Their revelry seems excessive. In fact, Alfred Edersheim notes that "it was deemed a religious duty to give pleasure to the newly married couple."[17] Instead of a functional, two-minute covenantal ceremony, we find festivities lasting a week or more.[18] The more pharisaical in every age could cry, "What waste!" while God's Word cries, "What joy!" Christ participated in at least one of these times of revelry, and He was directly instrumental in maintaining the festive spirit at the feast (John 2:1–11). The specifying of festive earthly conditions in Christ's coming kingdom, then, implies that at least some entertainments are the external reflection of righteous internal joy.

## The Admission of Pleasure in the Divine Character[19]

The Bible also testifies that God delights or takes pleasure in some things while not in others. After each day of creation, God observed His work and delighted in it (Gen. 1). God takes pleasure in righteousness and righteous ones (1 Chron. 29:17; Pss. 147:11; 149:4). This leads to His delighting in favoring and blessing His people, often even materially (Pss. 35:27; 36:8; Luke 12:32). His will and pleasure are closely intertwined to the extent that the doing of His will is His good pleasure (Isa. 53:10; Eph. 1:5, 9). On the other hand He never takes pleasure in sin or sinners (Ps. 5:4; Eccles. 5:4; Mal. 1:10), in the death of sinners (Ezek. 18:23, 32; 33:11), in ritualism without faith (Heb. 10:6, 8), or in unbelief (Heb. 10:38). Two additional verses most clearly demonstrate the pleasure of God with His people. Zephaniah 3:17 portrays God in

---

[17] *Sketches of Jewish Social Life in the Days of Christ* (Reprint, Grand Rapids: Eerdmans, 1972), 152.

[18] "The marriage festivities generally lasted a week, but the bridal days extended over a full month." Ibid., 155.

[19] John Piper's *The Pleasures of God: Meditations on God's Delight in Being God* (Sisters, OR: Multnomah, 2000) explores this theme in great detail.

terms of the exultant, triumphant warrior: "The Lord thy God in the midst of thee is mighty; he will save, he will rejoice over thee with joy; he will rest in his love, he will joy over thee with singing." Moreover, Isaiah 62:5 shows God's delighting in His people in a fashion that He has called analogous to a bridegroom at a wedding feast: "As the bridegroom rejoiceth over the bride, so shall thy God rejoice over thee." These last two verses present the joy of God in a manner that seems almost gratuitous. His actions are the actions of righteous festivity. The Scriptures indicate, then, that God delights not only in observing the effects of His own work but also in observing the righteous sub-creative activity of man.

A Christian worldview takes the testimony of God's Word in its context and explores how God intended people to operate in relation to their surroundings. It applies this testimony and the principles gained from the Word in our own context. And it lives for the glory of God in any generation.

## BIBLICAL DATA CONCERNING ENTERTAINMENT

Although the terms *entertainment, fun,* and *leisure* never occur in the English texts of the Bible, the concept of pleasure—as well as national and personal times of amusement and diversion from the work of ordinary life—occurs regularly.

The following terms and their cognates appear collectively over 1700 times in the English Bible (KJV): *dance* (26x), *drink* (364x), *eat* (734x), *feast* (145x), *play* (45x), *sing* (169x), *song* (92x), and *wine* (233x). While many of the references are to common activities (such as eating and drinking), the sheer volume of references attests man's natural connection with entertainment as previously defined. This count does not include references to music in general or to specific musical instruments, which add over 250 instances. In addition, *delight* (82x), *joy* (187x), *please* (104x), *pleasure* (68x), and *rejoice* (240x) add nearly 700 citations of emotional or cognitive response to circumstances. While many of these passages do not address entertainment, they add credibility to the assertion that a biblical philosophy of humanity must address man's righteous capacity for pleasure. These data stand beside just over 820 references to *work, labor, toil,* and their cognates. Warnings against specific negative uses of entertainment occur dozens of times in the Scriptures: *drunk* (77x), *glutton* (4x), *idle* (11x), *revel* (14x), *riot* (7x), *sloth/sluggard* (23x), and *wanton* (5x). Far from being underrepresented, the topic of entertainment occurs regularly in Scripture. The difficulty for us today comes in sorting out the legitimate use of entertainment and the parameters that bound its rightness in our generation.

These data, however, do not present a rigid picture of entertainment. Much like a balanced portrayal of entertainment today, the Bible records the existence of neutral, positive, and negative entertainment.

### Neutral References

Many passages simply assume that entertainment is occurring, without commenting positively or negatively on the entertainment itself. See, for example, Revelation 18:22: "And the voice of harpers, and musicians, and of pipers, and trumpeters, shall be heard no more at all in thee; and no craftsman, of whatsoever craft he be, shall be found any more in thee; and the sound of a millstone shall be heard no more at all in thee." The passage does not condemn entertainment but the city in which it was practiced. If entertainment *per se* were sinful, the passage would also be calling work evil. Instead, the passage communicates that Babylon's evil warranted a judgment so severe that her culture would perish entirely.

The following passages most closely align with the belief that entertainment is a natural part of humanity with a variety of purposes: rejoicing at victory (Judg. 11:34; 1 Sam. 18:6; 21:11; 29:5), rejoicing in the Lord (Judg. 21:21), rejoicing in the installation of a righteous king (2 Chron. 23:13), commemorating the past and remembering history and culture (1 Sam. 21:11; 29:5), contesting of strength and ability (2 Sam. 2:14),[20] rejoicing at the restoration of family (Luke 15:25), and pure amusement (Job 21:11–12; 41:5; Eccles. 2:8; 3:4; Dan. 6:18). Amos 6:5 is particularly instructive. Within the context of declaring woe upon those who are at ease in Zion, verse 5 addresses those "that chant to the sound of the viol, and invent to themselves instruments of musick, like David." The passage does not condemn the people for their musical entertainment; otherwise, it would have to condemn David as well. It observes the fact of cultural entertainment and does not critique it. Rather, the passage condemns the people for their entertainment-oriented mindset to the exclusion of all else. They spent all their time in self-gratification rather than being "grieved for the affliction of Joseph" (v. 6). In other words, their entertainment was out of place. It superseded and eradicated genuine spiritual sensitivity. Instead of accepting pleasure as from God's hand, the people treated pleasure as self-existing and self-warranting. They violated the biblical criteria of godly priorities and purposefulness outlined previously.

In the passages above, the actors were sometimes good and sometimes evil. The outcome was sometimes positive and sometimes negative, but the Bible never comments on the righteousness or

---

[20]This unusual passage illustrates the use of combat for entertainment. The Hebrew term שׂחק communicates the idea of sporting or playing. Joab and Abner, commanders of their respective armies under David and Ishbosheth, rested by the pool of Gibeon. Each side picked twelve men for the sparring match, and the commanders and armies watched the battle—apparently for the sake of diversion.

wickedness of the entertainment itself. For example, Isaiah 11 depicts conditions that exist in the millennial kingdom. All would agree that this is a time of great spiritual and physical blessing, yet verse eight comments on the playing of a child without positive or negative comment on the entertainment itself—"And the sucking child shall play on the hole of the asp, and the weaned child shall put his hand on the cockatrice' den." The verse communicates the security that will exist in the coming kingdom. The reader infers, rightly, that the child's playing is not likely evil, since the context is one of blessing, but the passage does not directly commend or condemn the playing. In addition, Paul repeatedly uses Roman entertainment as illustrations in his writing. He cites running (1 Cor. 9:24–27; Gal. 2:2; 2 Tim. 4:7; see also Heb. 12:1), a general competing in the games (1 Cor. 9:25; 2 Tim. 2:5), and boxing (1 Cor. 9:26). In addition he expresses acquaintance with some of the poetry and theatrical performances of his day in his citations of Epimenides of Crete (Acts 17:28; Titus 1:12), Aratus and/or Cleanthes (Acts 17:28), and Menander (1 Cor. 15:33). While he does not specifically encourage such entertainments, he does not treat them negatively. It is not at all likely, however, that he would have chosen sinful activities as representations of righteous Christian activity.

Entertainment is not the focal point of the preceding passages, but it does occur within their contexts. While one would hardly preach a sermon on entertainment derived from such statements, he should accept the naturalness and regularity of their occurrence as scriptural testimony to the innocuous quality of at least some forms of entertainment.

**Positive References**

Several passages indicate that a spiritually blessed condition is associated with purposeful entertainment. Particularly noteworthy here is the fact that natural, God-intended entertainments cease when the people suffer judgment and flourish when people experience God's blessing. In the middle of the ruin brought on Judah for her sin, Jeremiah cries, "The elders have ceased from the gate, the young men from their musick. The joy of our heart is ceased; our dance is turned into mourning" (Lam. 5:14–15). Obviously, if entertainment were evil, then Jeremiah would have no cause for mourning when it passed away. He should rejoice rather than grieve at the absence of amusement. However, the surrounding verses show uninterrupted, tedious labor to be a sign of God's curse on humanity, not of His blessing. This passage also indicates that entertainment really is a reflection of the heart condition. It portrays the joy of the soul by revelry.

Likewise, Isaiah cries, "And gladness is taken away, and joy out of the plentiful field; and in the vineyards there shall be no singing, neither shall there be shouting: the treaders shall tread out no wine in their presses; I have made their vintage shouting to cease" (16:10). The absence of the festivals that accompany harvest shows the presence of God's judgment on the nation.

When God reverses the curse under the New Covenant, He offers the following promises to His people: "Again I will build thee, and thou shalt be built, O virgin of Israel: thou shalt again be adorned with thy tabrets, and shalt go forth in the dances of them that make merry" (Jer. 31:4); "Then shall the virgin rejoice in the dance, both young men and old together: for I will turn their mourning into joy, and will comfort them, and make them rejoice from their sorrow" (Jer. 31:13); "And the streets of the city shall be full of boys and girls playing in the streets thereof" (Zech. 8:5). These passages indicate that some types of entertainment are the spontaneous overflow of joyful hearts, and the absence of such joy in the heart of a person indicates dire circumstances. These verses comment favorably on entertainment itself. If God intends to re-establish the joyous expression of pleasure in His kingdom,[21] then entertainment must not be inherently evil.

A few verses indicate the existence of a purposeful entertainment that is designed (either with or without effect) to produce spiritually beneficial results. When the servants of Saul sought out a man to play the harp before him, the objective was to soothe his troubled spirit. The people of Israel believed that entertainment could aid in producing refreshment, tranquility, and peace in the human spirit (1 Sam. 16:16–18, 23).

**Negative References**

Many passages exhibit clearly a negative attitude toward entertainment, but most of these contexts also include a reason for God's condemnation of the particular pleasure. God condemns many entertainments on the basis of their illegitimate sexual nature, their excessiveness, or their folly. Fallen man is often amused by that which is immoral. The people of Israel exhibited a desire for immoral pleasure in the wilderness when their feasting turned to idolatry and sexual perversion (Exod. 32:6; 1 Cor. 10:7). Herod's observing the dance of Salome apparently fits this pattern as well (Matt. 14:6; Mark 6:22).

First Peter 4:3 adds several bases for God's condemnation of certain forms of entertainment. "For the time past of our life may suffice us to have wrought the will of the Gentiles, when we walked in lasciviousness, lusts, excess of wine, revellings, banquetings, and abominable idolatries." *Lasciviousness* and *lusts* are general terms that include the sexual impurity already mentioned. The next three terms address two new issues—excess and a lack of control.

---

[21]References in the Old Testament prophets to days of pleasure include both Israel's restoration following the captivity and Israel's ultimate joy in the millennial kingdom.

All three terms indicate that people can distort God-given pleasure by a lack of control. The first term depicts an over-saturation with wine.[22] *Revellings* pertains to a party atmosphere that regularly attended the worship of false deities. These parties occurred "in honor of a god, particularly Bacchus, . . . ending usually in the party's sallying forth from their banqueting-room to parade the streets and indulge in whatever folly or wickedness suggested itself."[23] *Banquetings* refers to drinking parties that, by the time of the New Testament, were associated with excessive drinking. Entertainment must not rule us. God created us to exercise dominion over the earth. He did not create earthly things to exercise dominion over us. We must never give ourselves over to an atmosphere of pleasure to the extent that we lose control. Early Christians recognized that cruelty, violence, and inhumanity were not acceptable entertainments for believers. Brutality and suffering may amuse the unbeliever, but we who know Christ cannot treat them as pleasurable (Judg. 16:25–27).

Finally, the Bible condemns all forms of entertainment that engage in or amount to folly. The fool finds mischief amusing (Prov. 10:23). The fool delights in deceiving people for fun (Prov. 26:19; 2 Pet. 2:13). The foolish and perverse person pokes fun at the righteous and his God (Isa. 57:4).

These passages demonstrate that at least two scriptural grounds can disqualify entertainment as right for a believer. Entertainment that directly violates God's moral commands is never appropriate. And when we misuse pleasure in an excessive or uncontrolled

[22]D. Edmond Hiebert notes, "[οἰνοφλυγίαις], a term that occurs only here in the New Testament, denotes habitual drunkenness. The compound noun, composed of *oinos*, 'wine,' and the verb *phluō*, 'to bubble up, to overflow,' depicts one who is soaked to overflowing with wine." *1 Peter* (Chicago: Moody Press, 1992), 261.

[23]Robert Johnstone, *The First Epistle of Peter: Revised Text, with Introduction and Commentary* (Reprint, Minneapolis: James Family, 1978), 312.

fashion, it becomes improper even if the action itself is not inherently evil.

## Entertainment and Worship

Many verses address actions that appear to be entertaining in their effect but not in their motivation. These verses treat the purposeful use of singing, dancing, eating, and drinking for worship. Entertainment seeks relaxation and amusement intentionally as its basic purpose. Worship does not. God receives the attention of His people as they revel in His goodness. While rejoicing in the character of God, praising His person, and submitting to His will may result in physical rest, interest, and pleasure in the believer, these things are not his purpose in worship. Observing this truth, Dr. Dan Olinger noted, "Entertainment is for man's benefit, with man as the audience. Worship is for God's benefit, with God as the audience." And David F. Wells comments, "The purpose of worship is clearly to express the greatness of God and not simply to find inward release or, still less, amusement. Worship is theological rather than psychological."[24] A fundamental difference exists between entertainment and worship that should caution believers against the tendency to blend or equate the two.

The Bible does not depict the worship of God as somber in every case. There were times for singing, laughing, playing instruments, eating, and drinking before the Lord. These give *patterns* for legitimate entertainments, but they are not entertainments in themselves. Note particularly the following verses, which are representative of the joyful, delightful worship of God throughout Scripture:

---

[24]"A Tale of Two Spiritualities," in *Losing Our Virtue: Why the Church Must Recover Its Moral Vision* (Grand Rapids: Eerdmans, 1998), 40.

And Miriam the prophetess, the sister of Aaron, took a timbrel in her hand; and all the women went out after her with timbrels and with dances. (Exod. 15:20)

And it came to pass, as the ark of the covenant of the Lord came to the city of David, that Michal the daughter of Saul looking out at a window saw king David dancing and playing: and she despised him in her heart. (1 Chron. 15:29)

And David said unto Michal, It was before the Lord, which chose me before thy father, and before all his house, to appoint me ruler over the people of the Lord, over Israel: therefore will I play before the Lord. (2 Sam. 6:21)

Let them praise his name in the dance: let them sing praises unto him with the timbrel and harp. (Ps. 149:3)

Praise him with the timbrel and dance: praise him with stringed instruments and organs. (Ps. 150:4)

There can be no doubt from Scripture that the worship of God can be delightful to the believer, but the verses that address pleasure in worship do not set entertainment as the *goal* of worship. One cannot start with the presupposition that the worship of God is drab, boring, colorless, and lifeless and needs to be revved up by importing more appealing activities. Rather, one finds that in his worship of God he finds the spiritual rest, pleasure, and interest that he ultimately seeks and needs. In this sense worship cannot truly fit the category of entertainment.

How then do these passages serve as a pattern for entertainment? The fact that certain activities are prescribed or encouraged by God for worship and not forbidden to be used elsewhere indicates the possibility of their broader availability to us for pleasure. For instance, sacrifices were commanded by God but were restricted to the appropriate location, time, and office. The people were not to build high places and sacrifice on them, and God specifically rebuked their doing so. But there are no indications that the use of music and revelry outside of the worship setting are inappropriate. In fact, we have already shown through the customs of Israel that God tacitly approved of entertainment that was used within appropriate parameters.

## Summary

A survey of biblical passages concerning amusement has shown us the following:

- Entertainment of various forms occurs in Scripture.

- Sometimes entertainment is morally valuable.

- Sometimes entertainment is morally destructive.

- Entertainment and worship are distinct in purpose.

This leads us to conclude that our criteria proposed previously are truly important. We cannot simply ignore the question, and we must not misrepresent human amusement as either totally justified or totally condemned by Scripture. This leads us to consider in the next chapter where our thinking can run astray and cause us to fall into unbiblical extremes on our topic.

# 4

## WRONG PHILOSOPHIES OF
## ENTERTAINMENT

$I$f a theology of entertainment truly exists, one or more competing perspectives on entertainment likely exist in a fallen world.[1]
Satan counterfeits the operations of God. Where God creates legitimate, balanced, and moral pleasure, Satan substitutes illegitimate,
imbalanced, and immoral pleasure. Sometimes this fraud occurs
in the realm of human thinking. Satan wishes not only to pervert
the good things that God has made but also to deprive humanity of those good things. He depicts God falsely as an austere or
malignant Being Who is eager to see our ruin and misery. In the
realm of entertainment, Satan offers at least two extreme positions
that distort God's plan. These are libertinism and asceticism.

### LIBERTINISM

### Definition

We have a tendency to confuse libertinism with Christian liberty.
Christian liberty exists where several morally acceptable options
are available. Our liberty is the freedom to choose among these
righteous alternatives. It is not an open-ended freedom from all
constraint. Romans 6 rejects the libertine mindset on the basis of

---

[1]Several works address these competing perspectives on culture. See particularly H.
Richard Niebuhr, *Christ and Culture* (New York: Harper, 1951); D. A. Carson and
John D. Woodbridge, eds. *God and Culture: Essays in Honor of Carl F. H. Henry* (Grand
Rapids: Eerdmans, 1993). These books show how Christians have sometimes utterly re-
pudiated culture, have totally accepted culture, or have fallen somewhere between the
extremes. Many Christians assume the validity of one position against all the others.
Yet the Bible gives examples of different responses to culture depending on the morality of the specific cultural item being addressed.

the Christian's new life in Christ. If someone is dead to sin, he must not indulge in sin. Freedom from sin is freedom unto righteousness (Rom. 6:18–20). The two cannot coexist.

Then what is libertinism? In the realm of entertainment, it is the warping of biblical reality by the insistence that *all* entertainment is neutral or good.[2] In other words, it defines all options as morally acceptable. At its heart this type of thinking denies that Satan has perverted God's plan. It insists that restraint or limitation of any form of entertainment does not coincide with Christian freedom. Pop culture encourages this attitude, issuing an "invitation to moral autonomy" that people find hard to reject.[3] Libertinism asserts our independence and our right to decide ultimate questions for ourselves. In the realm of entertainment, it scoffs at tradition, authority, and high culture. For example, there are entertainers and artists who show deliberate contempt for traditions and conventions. They express hatred toward any restriction in the attempt to magnify their own creativity. And they challenge moral conventions by reordering the world around themselves.[4] They call their own artistry good while calling God's artistry evil. In this they invert the truth. Scripture describes this unbridled self-centeredness and inversion of truth as folly. Every disobedient act rests on the assumption that the existing authority has no right to restrain what we wish to do. Children touch breakable objects, run in the house, and throw their food, insisting on doing what they want. Students turn in papers late, eat in class, and break dress codes, insisting that school authorities have no right to tell them what to

---

[2]Philosophical libertinism advocates gratuitous change in standards and traditions, personal independence, and a questioning of all authorities. It is closely allied with modernism, yet it also appears in the attitudes of some Christian groups in Scripture. The church at Corinth depicts these qualities by its acceptance of sinful practices within the church and its repeated rejection of apostolic authority prior to Paul's severe letter.

[3]Myers, *All God's Children*, 69.

[4]Ibid., 112–13.

do. Citizens run red lights, evade taxes, and commit crimes, denying the government's right to order conduct. These violations are
obvious, but most people do not consider that their insistence on
personal liberty may be challenging the authority of God to define
right and wrong.[5]

## Biblical Refutation

Since God is perfectly free to define right and wrong, any challenge to His authority cannot succeed. Nabal provides a classic
example of a libertine attitude and its judgment (1 Sam. 25). This
foolish man took a libertine stance toward decency and courtesy.
He refused to show kindness toward others in a time of sheep
shearing, a traditional time of sharing and hospitality (vv. 7, 11).
He added to this folly his rejection of God's authority. He insulted
David (vv. 10–11) even though God had already appointed David
to be the next king of Israel in Saul's place. That this divine ap-
pointment was well known appears in Abigail's response to David
(vv. 30–31). It is no accident, then, that we should find in this fool
a fool's perspective on entertainment. He wined and dined exces-
sively and without constraint (v. 36). In the end his self-serving
redefinition of right and wrong brought divine retribution. God
struck him (v. 38).

God's Word responds to libertinism with a persistent appeal to heed
God's wisdom. In a lengthy passage depicting God as Judge, Psalm
50 warns the wicked against presumptuous declarations of right
and wrong. Those who claim to defend truth, justice, and righteousness while participating in and defending evil fall under severe
judgment (50:16–22). Modern entertainment culture contributes

---

[5]Citing a sermon of Puritan minister Joshua Moody, Daniels says, "'The people of
God are free to use the things of this life . . . for their convenience and comfort; but
yet he hath set bounds to this liberty, that it may not degenerate into licentiousness.'"
*Puritans at Play*, 7.

to this class of sin by creating new "virtues" of tolerance, relativism, and unbridled freedom. God will not allow a redefinition of His truth. His character will not change, and it is essential that we conform our amusements to His will.

## Practical Refutation

Libertinism does not offer a workable system since insistence on unconstrained freedom self-destructs in practice. One person's freedom to air commercials that sell an immoral product violates another person's freedom to live a life untainted by such commercials. The freedom to blast one's music at whatever volume one desires violates another's freedom to live a tranquil and peaceful life.[6] The freedom to post billboards and to placard indecent magazine covers where they are unavoidable violates another's freedom to live a life uncluttered by such indecency. Libertinism ultimately raises the question *liberty for whom*? It certainly cannot provide liberty for all people equally. God treats true liberty as that system which allows the righteous to live righteously. He specifically encourages His people to pray for a government that will permit such liberty to prevail (1 Tim. 2:2).

Libertinism also fails to obtain the happiness that it seeks. The mere pursuit of amusement cannot bring real joy to man.[7] His entertainment must be informed by and consonant with Scripture in order to produce a lasting joy. Since God created humanity to know and enjoy Himself forever, people cannot find ultimate hap-

---

[6]Medved provides a personal illustration in which his family's enjoyment of a public park was violated by a group of teens who arrived later playing rap music. When Medved asked the teens to turn the music down a little, one "offered a silent smirk and then cranked up the sound level even further." *Hollywood vs. America*, 269.

[7]Contrary to the impressions of some writers, the entertainment of the mind and body through hobbies cannot ultimately serve as "paths to happiness." Margaret E. Mulac offers some valuable observations on the nature of man, but she mistakes an abstract desire for pleasure for a humanity rightly related to God. *Hobbies: The Creative Use of Leisure* (New York: Harper & Brothers, 1959), 15–34.

piness in any form of entertainment that rejects God or His moral statutes. In order to bring genuine profit to a person, entertainment must stem from a heart that is righteously aligned with God.

## Summary

All our defenses of liberty should answer the important questions *liberty from what?* and *liberty unto what?* Our response should always coincide with Scripture's admonition to be progressively freed from the world and unto Christ (Rom. 12:1–2). With reference to our entertainment, we must be cautious about insisting on our personal liberty. Instead, we should base our amusement choices on a footing that is more firm than personal choice.[8] When God has spoken, other options are closed to us. We cannot use a misdefined liberty as a veiled attempt to free ourselves from God's standards.

The best defense against libertinism is informed obedience. We can live accidentally as libertines if we are ignorant of God's standards. But we are still culpable for our sin. An increasing number of Christians fall into this category as the knowledge of God's Word declines in American culture. Entertainment itself plays an important role in sapping the time and energy needed to study Scripture adequately, and that absence of study produces believers who are progressively weaker in making wise entertainment choices. The moral and logical relativism of the age makes persuading others concerning the truth increasingly difficult. Immature Christians have been taught by their culture to reject higher claims to authority. They view any restriction of personal freedom as the imposition of the opinions of Puritanical leaders, even where such a

---

[8]"The fact that there have been different opinions about good and bad in different times and places in no way proves that none is superior to others. . . . On the face of it, the difference of opinion would seem to raise the question as to which is true or right rather than to banish it." Allan Bloom, *The Closing of the American Mind* (New York: Simon & Schuster, 1987), 39.

restriction has clear basis in Scripture. They often respond with false accusations, as the Corinthian church reacted to Paul. Some cannot discern between the wise counsel of mature believers and the foolish advice of their peers. Ultimately God's Word provides the answer to such libertine thinking and acting. To escape this particular distortion of biblical truth, we must thoroughly search the Scriptures and commit ourselves to obedience.

## ASCETICISM

### Definition

Asceticism refers to the way of thinking that forbids for oneself (and often insists on prohibiting for others) many actions and pleasures permitted by Scripture. The specific form of asceticism that makes keeping the law a prerequisite for salvation is not in view here. The term *Pharisaism* adds the implication of hypocrisy that is not always present in the ascetic. A pejorative use of the terms *Pietism* or *Puritanism* would misrepresent the groups that they stand for. While it is true that many Pharisees, Puritans, and Pietists would reject the use of entertainment, they are not identical with such a rejection.[9] *Asceticism*, then, is the best term to describe the denying of our right to participate in entertainment. Asceticism aligns itself philosophically with Stoicism as well as with various mild forms of dualism. Each of these belief systems claims that amusements and physical pleasures are inherently evil.[10] The biblical labels that Paul

[9]In fact, Bruce Daniels observes that "the Puritan ideal of leisure and recreation contained a profound ambivalence. Puritans had trouble articulating their ideal of appropriate leisure and recreation." *Puritans at Play*, xiii.

[10]Some forms of dualism actually moved in the opposite direction and justified all manner of material pleasures and evils due to the transience of material things. Paul contends against such a philosophy as well in 1 Cor. 6:12–20.

gives to those who profess this philosophy include "weak in the faith" (Rom. 14:1) and "weak" (Rom. 14:2; 15:1).[11]

## Biblical Refutation

Asceticism warps biblical reality by insisting that most, if not all, entertainment is evil. We have already seen biblical evidence that entertainment may have a righteous purpose. Asceticism assumes that we are most spiritual when we are rejecting certain parts of the created order. In condemning the sinful excesses of many forms of entertainment, it often creates the new excess of a falsely defined piety.

Asceticism recognizes the sinful nature of man, his tendency toward self-gratification, and the alliance of the world system against God.[12] Its representatives include a cautious group of believers who are not to be mocked or mistreated.[13] The Bible commands the strong believer to "receive" this weak one in a manner calculated to avoid offending him and to limit the stirring up of controversy. Rather, it requires charity from the strong (1 Cor. 8:1). Paul rebukes those who are weak in faith only when they begin to overreach their

---

[11]Note that Paul uses the term *weak* in 1 Cor. 8 to describe those who are willing to offend their consciences by doing that which they believe to be wrong, because their conscience is "weak." The use in 1 Corinthians appears to differ from the use in Romans.

[12]Often this recognition stemmed from a philosophical reaction to former religion and practice. "Some pagans were so repelled by the self-indulgence they saw as an integral part of the world in which they lived that they turned from it all and lived ascetic lives." Leon Morris, *The Epistle to the Romans*, The Pillar New Testament Commentary (Grand Rapids: Eerdmans, 1988), 477.

[13]Morris notes that in Rom. 14:1 Paul "does not mean a person who trusts Christ but little, the man of feeble faith. Rather, the person he has in mind is the one who does not understand the conduct implied by faith" (ibid.). A scornful response from the strong in faith does not reflect the pure love that Christ made central to His body, especially since, as Charles Hodge observes, "this weakness is not inconsistent with piety." *A Commentary on Romans*, A Geneva Series Commentary (1835; reprint, Great Britain: Mackays of Chatham, 1989), 416.

knowledge and consequently begin to legislate right and wrong for other believers.

Although Scripture calls for charity from the strong, it also encourages the weak to grow in knowledge. The remaining context of Romans 14 reasons from the facts of salvation that the strong hold the more theologically correct position although they must practice love. Paul's explanation and defense of the viewpoint of the strong believer encourages the weak to come to a right understanding of Christ's sacrifice. The ascetic mentality that insists on cutting off God-given, natural pleasures actually caricatures life. It engages in an over-scrutinizing of life that minutely categorizes all things. This truncates God's plan for mankind by lopping off part of what humanity was created to be. It has the appearance of spirituality while offering a fractured reality. Note particularly Colossians 2:16–23:

> Let no man therefore judge you in meat, or in drink, or in respect of an holyday, or of the new moon, or of the sabbath days: which are a shadow of things to come; but the body is of Christ. Let no man beguile you of your reward in a *voluntary humility* and worshipping of angels, intruding into those things which he hath not seen, vainly puffed up by his fleshly mind, and not holding the Head, from which all the body by joints and bands having nourishment ministered, and knit together, increaseth with the increase of God. Wherefore *if ye be dead with Christ from the rudiments of the world, why, as though living in the world, are ye subject to ordinances, (touch not; taste not; handle not; which all are to perish with the using;) after the commandments and doctrines of men? Which things have indeed a shew of wisdom in will worship, and humility, and neglecting of the body; not in any honour to the satisfying of the flesh.*

The "voluntary humility" in verse 18 is a common biblical word for humility.[14] Normally humility is a commendable Christian virtue, but the context in Colossians indicates a different use of the term. Verse 23 shows us that the "humility" of the ascetic is not true humility. It is a self-abasement by human definition rather than by God's definition. It has the appearance of wisdom and great piety but lacks both. Genuine humility is submission to the authority of God. When God gives a command, true humility responds with swift obedience. When God gives latitude for human choice, true humility responds with grateful use of the freedom. It does not forbid what God allows nor allow what God forbids. The restrictions of verse 21, "touch not, taste not, handle not," are not a reflection of God's attitude toward the created world. They are a distortion of truth.

To focus entirely on what we *are* while neglecting what we *were created to be* distorts the biblical perspective of man.[15] True, we are prone to sin. We should guard ourselves carefully against the sinful entertainments of this world, but the argument does not follow logically that we should thereby exclude all pleasures in this life. Such reasoning actually succumbs to a false view of divine-human conflict proposed by Satan. The Adversary juxtaposes God's interest and man's interest and asserts that they are contradictory. He claims that human pleasure and God's will conflict. Satan continues to say to mankind, "Your good and God's good are mutually exclusive," while God says, "Your good and My good are inextricably linked."

---

[14]The term is ταπεινοφροσύνη, which occurs in important passages such as Eph. 4:2; Phil. 2:3; and 1 Pet. 5:5 as a virtue. In fact, Col. 3:12 commissions believers to "put on . . . humility [ταπεινοφροσύνη]."

[15]See C. S. Lewis, "Learning in War-Time" in *The Weight of Glory and Other Addresses*, rev. ed. (New York: Macmillan, 1980), 20–23.

Asceticism often creates a scapegoat from a particular form of entertainment. Some crusades against radio, television, and computer games have implied that all the woes of culture are due solely or primarily to the influence of a specific entertainment. For instance, Edmund Pearson notes that "parents who had shamefully neglected a son and allowed him to stray into mischief found it very convenient to stand in a police court and lay all the blame on dime novels. Inherent deviltry; neglect; selfishness; cruel egotism—oh, dear, no. It was nothing but wicked dime novels. Willy was such a good boy until he began to read them. . . . Judges and teachers and clergymen and Sunday-school superintendents and even police chiefs began to denounce dime novels. It was the most useful explanation of crime, and the easiest excuse for the offender."[16] This attribution of vice to a single modern cause contradicts the Bible. Scripture shows us that sin stems from our fallen condition (Rom. 5:12–19) and that we sin because we are sinners (Mark 7:18–23). While we must avoid the evil influence of the world, and we cannot justify any participation in what is actually sinful, we must not pretend that erecting barriers against all amusement will solve our sin problem.

Romans 7 illustrates another weakness of the ascetic mindset. The law provokes sin. Some law is necessary, but the creating of many rules and regulations actually stirs up sin by adding to every moral offense the additional sin of lawbreaking. Moreover, sinful human nature resists law, especially where the law seems overly restrictive or unnecessary. The ascetic multiplies regulations in the attempt to avoid sin, but he actually creates more sins that he can commit. Once he has defined an entertainment as inherently sinful, he cannot participate without breaking the law. If God has defined the entertainment to be evil, then he has done well to concur with His

[16]*Dime Novels* (Boston: Little, Brown, 1929), 46.

standard; but if the standard is man-made, the codification of law merely results in greater opportunity for sin.

## Practical Refutation

Although asceticism is present in every generation, some eras struggle with it more than others. For example, the tendency to reject entertainment and pleasure grew to extreme proportions during the early nineteenth-century Victorian era. The strictness of that century exceeded the narrowness of the Puritans who preceded it. The amusements forbidden as devilish included bowling, bicycle riding, croquet, roller skating, baseball, football, chess, tennis, and "fairs and picnics, even under church auspices."[17] But the prudishness of the Victorian era did not solve the moral problems of society.

This failure demonstrates that asceticism is invalid on the practical level. First, it replaces an authoritative biblical code of ethics with manmade regulations. Manmade ethics lack the power of absolute truth. Recognizing their hollowness, we eventually resist those ethics as unjustified limitations of our personal freedom. We chafe against "tradition" when its merit runs no deeper than the personal opinions of the previous generation. Second, asceticism produces multiple standards that all claim absolute authority. We are overwhelmed by the competing claims. Instead of searching for what is true absolutely, we are reduced to defending our own personal set of ascetic ideals as true. Or worse, we despair at the multiplicity of the competing claims and begin to deny that a real standard exists.

## Summary

Instead of offering additional competing authorities to our congregations and our children, it would be far better to show them where the biblical lines of right and wrong *must* apply uniformly to

---

[17]Ralph Slovenko and James A. Knight, *Motivations in Play, Games and Sport* (Springfield, IL: Charles C. Thomas, 1967), 121–32.

everyone. We can then show them where we have *chosen* to apply a biblical principle to our own particular circumstance.

For example, asceticism simply declares, "Computer games are evil, and television is morally indefensible." It then tries to defend its thesis and becomes angry or abusive when others do not agree. It has over-generalized concerning an entire class of actions. Biblical wisdom would argue that perpetrating unjustified violence is evil (Gen. 6:11–13; Pss. 11:5; 73:6; Jer. 22:3), blaspheming God's name is wicked (Exod. 20:7; Lev. 24:16; Job 2:9–10; Isa. 37:23ff.), and participating in immorality is contrary to Christ (1 Cor. 6:9, 18–20). We can then declare with biblical authority that *Grand Theft Auto* is morally evil and will not be permitted in our houses, since it is devoted to illicit violence. We can state on the basis of Scripture that certain television programs,[18] for example, are depraved and have no part in the Christian life, since they curse God and glorify immorality. We can then show our children how we have chosen to limit or avoid certain other games and programs because of their partial connections with evil (2 Cor. 6:14–7:1) or because they tend toward a violation of more general principles.

We should rejoice in natural, God-given pleasure. Unfortunately, in a fallen world the unnatural pleasure of sin has disfigured the natural. In attacking ungodly pleasure, we run the risk of attacking the godly pleasure it masquerades to be. We must avoid misrepresenting biblical truth by creating our own definitions of right and wrong. The best defense against asceticism is a conscious serving of Christ in a newness of spirit (Rom. 7:6), being led by the Holy Spirit (Rom. 8:1–16). This will involve us in carefully, scripturally evaluating our activities without creating new laws of conduct that supersede God's standard of righteousness.

---

[18]A common illustration at the time of writing was the TV drama *Desperate Housewives*; broadcast schedules being what they are, the examples need constant updating.

# 5

## TEST CASES FOR ENTERTAINMENT

### CHRISTIAN LIBERTY

Having examined our entertainment in light of specific biblical parameters, we may now run our entertainment choices through several general biblical sieves to test how well they honor Christ. Christian liberty serves as the first of these broad tests of the legitimacy of our amusements.[1]

Two New Testament passages provide data on Christian liberty: Romans 14–15 and 1 Corinthians 8–10. These passages yield several important observations. First, each passage addresses some form of cultural participation that Paul affirms in principle but is willing to limit in practice (Rom. 14:2, 5, 14; 1 Cor. 8:4; 10:23, 27). In order to avoid causing other believers to sin, the Christian must be willing to limit his legitimate freedom voluntarily. Even having acknowledged the biblical warrant for entertainment, we should be willing to restrict our actions when we know that they would encourage our brothers in Christ to violate their consciences.

Second, Paul asserts the real existence of Christian liberty. He also defends those who live out their God-given freedom as possessing the stronger position (Rom. 14:3–4, 6–9, 17–18; 1 Cor. 8:4–6, 10:25). Christian liberty is not a human construct. It is not the creation of a few Christian libertines. In application to our topic, we should note that Christian liberty affirms the valid place of entertain-

---

[1]See Randy Jaeggli, *Love, Liberty, and Christian Conscience* (Greenville, SC: Bob Jones University Press, 2007), for a thorough discussion of this topic.

ment, since God is the author of all good things, including human pleasure.

Third, in each case liberty applies only to non-moral issues. This is not to say that the choice we make has no moral consequence or does not touch morality in any way, but that the action in question finds no prohibition in Scripture. The action does not contradict the character of God. Paul uses illustrations of eating and drinking, but not of morality and immorality. He never makes a case for Christian liberty where such "liberty" violates a clear command of Scripture. It is essential that we evaluate our entertainment by the Bible to discern its rightness. Where God has forbidden an action, we cannot view it as entertainment. We cannot amuse ourselves with sin.

Fourth, Paul observes that the liberty issue neither brings a person closer to God nor pushes him further from God (Rom. 14:8, 22; 1 Cor. 8:8, 10:31). It does not defile him, nor does it improve him.[2] In other words, some facets of created humanity simply exist. Their theological importance derives not from their connection with some overarching moral principle but from their connection with God's creativity and right to define humanity. Truly legitimate entertainments do not create either piety or evil in themselves. It is our response that is pious or evil.

Fifth, Paul spends the majority of space and effort stimulating peace and unity within righteous diversity. He encourages reserved judgment (Rom. 14:4, 10), forethought (Rom. 14:13; 1 Cor. 8:9–13), love (Rom. 14:15; 1 Cor. 8:1), edification (Rom. 14:19–21; 15:1–3; 1 Cor. 8:9–13; 10:24), peace (Rom. 14:19; 1 Cor. 10:32), well-rooted faith (Rom. 14:22), and purity of conscience (Rom.

---

[2]This re-addresses the limited value of entertainment. Since it does not bring him closer to God, a believer should use it sparingly and appropriately.

14:23; 1 Cor. 8:7; 10:28–29). The believer's actions and reactions in response to brothers who disagree may have significant spiritual consequences. Greater issues are at stake than personal opinion or pleasure. This warns us against judging or scorning other Christians who have different entertainment standards. Our relationship with them must involve a righteous, loving, edifying, peace.

How then should we respond to these Scriptures? We should test our amusements against God's standard of righteousness, rejoice in God's marvelous design in permitting them for mankind, recognize their limited value, and limit ourselves in a manner calculated to avoid causing others spiritual harm wherever possible.[3]

## ECCLESIASTES

Solomon's exploration of life in Ecclesiastes yields powerful insight into fallen, frustrated, sinful humanity. It also addresses humanity as it was created to be. The barrenness of fallen human thinking appears in its seeking fulfillment in things of this world. Instead it finds frustration and futility. God did not create us to live *for* knowledge (1:13, 16–18; 2:12–17), pleasure (2:1, 10), drinking (2:3), construction and creation (2:4–6), accumulation (2:7–8; 4:8; 5:10, 13; 6:2–3), sexuality (2:8), labor (2:10–11, 18–23; 4:4, 8), passing on an inheritance (2:18–21), rule and dominion (4:1), or appetite (6:7). Solomon spends a great portion of the book demonstrating that although we lack control over our circumstances and do not know the future, we must do right in spite of life's uncertainty. Sometimes the wicked live well, and the righteous poorly. Sometimes base men and servants reign while kings grovel.

---

[3]Paul's statement in Rom. 14:22 could apply to entertainment choices in our not proclaiming our entertainment choices loudly. There is no need for us to do so. If we have truly weighed those choices biblically and have confidence that we could answer for them in the judgment, we do not need to persuade everyone else to our position. We most certainly must not boast about our liberty in a manner that damages our weaker brothers in faith.

Sometimes the fool is exalted while the wise are ignored. However, God retains control of all of life. What He has appointed for us should be used and enjoyed in right measure and within His set boundaries. All of those acts and qualities of life that cannot serve as our chief end have value, nonetheless, when appropriated rightly.[4] The attitude of the wise is not the hedonistic "Eat, drink, and be merry, for tomorrow we die," but the biblical "Eat, drink, and enjoy life as God has appointed."

The impression that Ecclesiastes is empty of theological value except in its conclusion overlooks several crucial thoughts. First, God is the author of all good pleasure. That we have badly distorted this legitimate pleasure does not negate God's original purpose and design. "Lo, this only have I found, that God hath made man upright; but they have sought out many inventions" (Eccles. 7:9). If God is the Creator of righteous pleasure, then He intends for us to experience that pleasure. We should enjoy all things that God has made within the boundaries that He has set. Yet Ecclesiastes demonstrates throughout that we can find satisfaction ultimately in God alone. This dual strand—ultimate satisfaction in God coupled with immediate delight in the pleasures He has created—presents a balanced picture of real humanity. Solomon uses a refrain to intertwine these two strands.[5]

---

[4]J. Stafford Wright, "Ecclesiastes," 5:1144–46 in *The Expositor's Bible Commentary*, ed. Frank E. Gaebelein (Grand Rapids: Zondervan, 1991).

[5]Solomon also argues these strands separately. In some cases he demonstrates the bankruptcy of human endeavor apart from God and the satisfaction that one finds only in God: "I have seen the travail, which God hath given to the sons of men to be exercised in it. He hath made every thing beautiful in his time: also he hath set the world in their heart, so that no man can find out the work that God maketh from the beginning to the end" (3:10–11). "For he shall not much remember the days of his life; because God answereth him in the joy of his heart" (5:20). "In the day of prosperity be joyful, but in the day of adversity consider: God also hath set the one over against the other, to the end that man should find nothing after him" (7:14). In other cases he demonstrates man's legitimate delight in pleasures: "Go thy way, eat thy bread with joy, and drink thy wine with a merry heart; for God now accepteth thy works" (9:7).

| Ref. | Refrain |
|------|---------|
| 2:24 | There is nothing better for a man than that he should eat and drink, and that he should make his soul enjoy good in his labour. This also I saw, that it was **from the hand of God**. |
| 2:26 | For **God giveth** to a man that is good in his sight wisdom, and knowledge, and joy. |
| 3:13 | And also that every man should eat and drink, and enjoy the good of all his labour, it is the **gift of God**. |
| 5:18–19 | Behold that which I have seen: it is good and comely for one to eat and to drink, and to enjoy the good of all his labour that he taketh under the sun all the days of his life, which **God giveth** him: for it is his portion. Every man also to whom **God hath given** riches and wealth, and hath given him power to eat thereof, and to take his portion, and to rejoice in his labour; this is the **gift of God**. |
| 8:15 | Then I commended mirth, because a man hath no better thing under the sun, than to eat, and to drink, and to be merry: for that shall abide with him of his labour the days of his life, which **God giveth** him under the sun. |

Each occurrence of the refrain depicts God as the giver of pleasure. *He* grants eating, drinking, enjoying of labor, wisdom, knowledge, joy, riches, wealth, merriness, and days of life. These refrains follow sections in which Solomon experiments with various human philosophies. In each case he concludes that satisfaction cannot be found in any human perspective. Trust in asceticism or self-deprivation is just as empty as faith in pleasure. Confidence in human knowledge or work is as misplaced as reliance on personal comfort. Those who complain against Solomon's argument evince their own theological imperfection. It is not piety but false human philosophy that rejects pleasure, since God is the Giver of real pleasure. It is not piety but sinful humanity that idolizes pleasure, since God is the Creator worthy of worship.

Second, Solomon observes that no one can comprehend all the purposes of God.

> Then I beheld all the work of God, that a man cannot find out the work that is done under the sun: because though a man labour to seek it out, yet he shall not find it; yea further; though a wise man think to know it, yet shall he not be able to find it. (8:17)

> As thou knowest not what is the way of the spirit, nor how the bones do grow in the womb of her that is with child: even so thou knowest not the works of God who maketh all. (11:5)

We do not have to understand to obey. We cannot fathom all aspects of the created order or of theological truth. We do not need to be able to plumb the philosophic depths of amusement in order to rejoice in pleasure. This fact should produce in us humility in our response to entertainment. We may not comprehend why God has allowed diversion and leisure to exist, but we can accept God's design and obey God's will. The attempt to press our knowledge beyond the revelation God has given results in frustration. It also leads to the creation of human philosophy. When theologians debate about unrevealed things, they attain not knowledge but speculation (1 Tim. 6:4; 2 Tim. 2:23; Titus 3:9). When we insist that God must loathe a certain human activity though His thoughts are hidden, we offer conjectures, not facts. Knowledge of good and evil rests on revelation. Where revelation permits a pleasure due to its part in God's created plan, none should despise it. Where revelation prohibits a pleasure as going beyond God's created plan, none should participate in it. Where revelation is silent, we may extrapolate the right course of action, but we must extrapolate humbly and wisely. No one knows why God created us to live ordinary lives of eating, drinking, sleeping, playing, communicating, and working, but we ought not think that we have entered into some profound wisdom when we exclude some facet of genuine humanity from our lives.

Third, Solomon reasons from these propositions that we must live normal lives in the fear of God.

> I know that, whatsoever God doeth, it shall be for ever: nothing can be put to it, nor any thing taken from it: and God doeth it, that men should fear before him. (3:14)

> I said in mine heart, God shall judge the righteous and the wicked: for there is a time there for every purpose and for every work. (3:17)

> For in the multitude of dreams and many words there are also divers vanities: but fear thou God. (5:7)

> It is good that thou shouldest take hold of this; yea, also from this withdraw not thine hand: for he that feareth God shall come forth of them all. (7:18)

> Though a sinner do evil an hundred times, and his days be prolonged, yet surely I know that it shall be well with them that fear God, which fear before him: but it shall not be well with the wicked, neither shall he prolong his days, which are as a shadow; because he feareth not before God. (8:12–13)

When we read Ecclesiastes, we should not conclude that we are to live an artificial humanity that denies pleasure. In fact, the artificial, self-made righteousness of Ecclesiastes 7:16 ruins, rather than rewards, a man.

> Be not righteous over much; neither make thyself over wise: why shouldest thou destroy thyself?[6]

Instead we must live an authentic humanity that delights in pleasure while constraining that pleasure with the fear of the Lord.

Every father who has taken his children to the seashore understands this principle. He sets his children down and watches merrily as his daughter runs shrieking down to the water's edge. He smiles as his toddling son plops down and digs in the sand. He observes their movements, their energy, their creativity, and his heart fills with delight in seeing his children pleased—knowing that he is the author of this vacation and the giver of the pleasure. Yet he also expects them to retain their fear of him in the midst of pleasure.[7] When he commands them to return to his side, he expects obedience regardless of how long or how intensely they have been enjoying themselves. He experiences profound enjoyment in giving them pleasure, but he never relinquishes authority or right over them. Ecclesiastes reveals this to be God's plan in giving pleasure to man.

---

[6]Solomon's statement does not repudiate genuine holiness. No one can attain perfection, and none can overreach righteousness. Rather his statement warns against a legalistic mentality that offers a standard of righteousness higher than God's own standard. This can occur in the discussion of human entertainment. Some postulate a strict standard of morality that makes all leisure sinful, but such a standard does not approximate real righteousness. It destroys a person through at least two means. First, once he sets the standard, he must keep it until his conscience itself repudiates the false standard. If he fails to keep his standard, he actually sins even though the standard itself was not God's standard of righteousness. Second, when he sets an unreasonable and unjustifiable standard of righteousness, others will reject him. They will scorn his "wisdom" as narrow-minded opinion and will withdraw from his beliefs and his company.

[7]A father also defends his children zealously. Because he loves his children, he acts forcefully to protect them from dangers such as drowning or shark attack. A loving father delights in giving pleasure, but a loving father also guards his child from being so caught up in the distractions of pleasure that he engages in harmful actions.

Rejoice, O young man, in thy youth; and let thy heart cheer thee in the days of thy youth, and walk in the ways of thine heart, and in the sight of thine eyes: but know thou, that for all these things God will bring thee into judgment. (11:9)

Let us hear the conclusion of the whole matter: Fear God, and keep his commandments: for this is the whole duty of man. For God shall bring every work into judgment, with every secret thing, whether it be good, or whether it be evil. (12:13–14)

A submissive Christian perception of entertainment strives to know God's perspective and to implement it with wisdom.[8] In answering the hard questions of life, we may disagree on particulars, but we must not disagree in the main. God is holy. God created us. God will judge.[9] He does not call us to be other than human, but He requires us to be made righteous through Christ and to live righteously in Christ. He does not esteem false spirituality or admire a piety that rejects what He calls good. Neither does He justify carelessness, apathy, or unchecked freedom. We who know the Lord must operate within these parameters for all our choices of life. We must submit to God on the issue of entertainment.

---

[8]Derek Kidner notes this emphasis on divinely guided, wise humanity: "The blunt 'Thou shalt' or 'shalt not' of the Law, and the urgent 'Thus saith the Lord' of the Prophets, are now joined by the cooler comments of the teacher and the often anguished questions of the learner. Where the bulk of the Old Testament calls us simply to obey and believe, this part of it . . . summons us to think hard as well as humbly; to keep our eyes open, to use our conscience and our common sense, and not to shirk the most disturbing questions." *The Wisdom of Proverbs, Job & Ecclesiastes* (Downers Grove, IL: InterVarsity, 1985), 11.

[9]Myers says, "There is one reality, ordered by the one God. We are answerable to Him for our conduct within that reality. Our cultural life should encourage us to acknowledge that reality and its center in Jesus Christ, not in our[selves]" (101).

## TELEVISION AS AN EXAMPLE: APPLYING
## BIBLICAL CRITERIA AND TEST CASES

It lies beyond the scope of this paper to address every form of entertainment in detail. The biblical worldview in the preceding pages is more valuable than one man's assessment of a specific type of amusement. A biblical worldview has an eternal quality that allows it to address changing circumstances. Specific forms of entertainment are often limited to a few years' duration. However, one form of entertainment—television—has seized the collective consciousness of the present age and dominates all others as the primary amusement. It serves as a proving ground for the preceding criteria, and it allows a brief survey of our application of biblical principles to entertainment choices.

We can go too far in describing the peculiar horrors of a particular form of entertainment, but television has clearly become a modern idol. It absorbs a disproportionate amount of our time and attention. We find it very easy to misuse television entertainment. Through it, people have contrived new means of carrying out the age-old sins of humanity (Eccles. 7:29; Jer. 4:22; Rom. 1:30). Rather than serving as inventors of and participants in evil, we must follow biblical criteria in creating and viewing television programs.

When measured against the principle of conformity to Christ, television often fares poorly. Even the most benign of programs can leave us more like the world than like the Lord. Game shows, like Roman and Greek games long before them, may emphasize human pride (in a competitor's or observer's intellect, power, skill, or courage), a sense of luck (contradicting the providence or sovereignty of God), and greed. Yet we can appreciate skill and knowledge without serving them or idolizing them. Christians have had to do so for millennia in their interaction with other games and sports. Nature programs, like Oriental religions before them, drip evolution and humanism—omitting altogether the proper sense of awe and wonder at the Creator. Yet we can observe the beauty of God's engineering through a biblically informed aesthetic and moral eye. We can point our children to God's majesty and wisdom in forming the world and its creatures. Cartoons often emphasize buffoonery and violence. Yet some serve the part of riddles and parables in their commentary on culture. Prime-time programs typically undermine the family, the church, and the government as inept, outdated, and unsophisticated institutions that we need not obey. Yet some provide at least a partially correct worldview in their support of God-ordained order. In other words, we must exercise vigilant discernment in our choices, and we must take care to give our children biblical perspective on entertainment. These deficiencies should not surprise us. Most producers, directors, actors, and advertisers have an entirely different agenda from God's. They are interested in communication as a commodity—as a money-making device. He is interested in communication as a means to the Way, the Truth, and the Life. Again, this contrast means that we need to watch television with carefulness and highly selective viewing lest we become more like the world than like Christ. We must evaluate our television viewing on the basis of its alignment with the character and work of Jesus Christ. We must never delight in that which degrades truth or contradicts God's Word.

Much of what appears on television violates the biblical criterion of purity. Television's insistence on holding man's attention predisposes it to act in a manner consistent with sinful humanity. Ratings drive advertising revenue. Revenue drives production. Entertainment drives the ratings. Appeals to prurient interests drive the entertainment. "ABC's *Desperate Housewives* is the most popular broadcast-network television show with kids aged 9–12 according to Nielsen stats."[10] As Kyle Haselden observes, "Sex itself does not have to be sold; therefore it is used to sell other things."[11] Hollywood experimented briefly with the Production Code of the 1930s, which drastically reduced incidences of sex and violence in the media, but the unending pursuit of profit led to a complete repudiation of the code in the 1970s.

Television relies most heavily on its visual image. The image itself must appeal to the broadest possible spectrum of people in order to increase its ratings. The broadest possible appeal that can be made to fallen humanity is based on our universal sinful inclination. Consequently, television is usually successful in capturing interest and maintaining an audience by depicting sin. Again, this should not surprise us: the world system does not love the Lord; it does not pursue His holiness. This means that we must walk very carefully in this life in order to maintain purity of heart before the Lord. The fact that society approves of impurity does not shift that standard for us.

Television tends to isolate people from one another and from a legitimate response to problems. Its programming elicits fear, anger, horror, sympathy, compassion, and love, then paradoxically encourages the viewer to suppress constructive activity associated with these emotions. Television does not want its observer to be incensed at evil, turn off the screen, and go do something productive to stop the evil. In a sense it says, "See how terrible this is? Now stay tuned and see even greater horrors." The regular viewer feels anger at the injustice and inhumanity presented on the screen, but he cannot solve the problem. In fact, in many cases there is often no real problem to be solved, since the setting is fictional. The viewer

---

[10]Parents Television Council, "Facts and TV Statistics," *parentstv.org*, http://www.parentstv.org/PTC/facts/mediafacts.asp; accessed 28 May 2007.

[11]*Morality*, 109.

experiences passion and love but does not respond constructively in showing mercy toward others. Romanowski observes, "The cinema experience allows for anonymity and safety; you feel no responsibility for what takes place in that world, although you may be affected emotionally and have opinions about it."[12] Television conditions the viewer to emote while failing to act constructively on that emotion.

Worse still, television often teaches a philosophy of immediate gratification and self-service that contradicts God's Word. Although this quality can be true of any entertainment, television is notoriously seductive in this realm. The viewer follows the storyline, experiences entertainment, and walks away concurring with humanism.[13] He rejoices when the hero takes matters into his own hands, seeks out the criminals, and kills them extra-judicially. He applauds when the poor, downtrodden prostitute meets a man who first participates in her trade but who grows to "really" love her. He responds with outrage when the "system" arrests the poor father who held up a convenience store to provide for his sick wife and three children. He excuses the shoplifting, substance abusing "foibles" of his favorite star, since it was the pressure that made her do it. The visual stimulus overrides both rational and spiritual objections and can indoctrinate people with worldly philosophy. Marvin Olasky notes, "Yes, Hollywood's fixation on sex must be fought, but at the same time we should note the deeper danger: Consumers of popular culture, including Christians, are often subtly conditioned to oppose transcendental reality and objective truth."[14] The viewer starts seeking instant emotional gratification

---

[12] *Eyes Wide Open*, 67.

[13] See Romanowski's argument and summary of the support of this point from other writers (ibid., 64).

[14] "Studying Babylon" in *Whirled Views: Tracking Today's Cultural Storms* (Wheaton, IL: Crossway, 1997), 102.

even where that gratification repudiates the Word of God. Commercials solicit human desire to an even greater extent than regular programming. While the regular programming tries to retain the viewer's attention so he will "stay tuned" for the commercials, the commercials exist for the purpose of stimulating discontent and a desire for immediate gratification. Coleen Cook asserts, "The very nature of television, which thrives on creating discontent for the sake of commercial prosperity, flies in the face of biblical commands."[15] These appeals to immediate gratification diminish the sense of forethought and eternity that are crucial to a biblical understanding of God, man, and coming judgment.

Television can attack truth from a position of stealth. Even if a particular program is morally good, the commercials may defile the mind. Even if a particular series has a track record of cleanness, one program may destroy the whole. Christian viewers find the rapid-fire attack on righteousness difficult to cope with. The problem becomes more difficult due to the hypnotic effect of television. In an interview with Dr. Erik Peper, Jerry Mander learned that television conditions people not to react to stimuli.[16] This produces a potentially lethal situation for the spiritual life of the believer. Television conditions him not to react and then depicts what he ought not watch. Peper observed, "The horror of television . . . is that the information goes in, but we don't react to it. . . . When you watch television you are training yourself not to react and so later on, you're doing things without knowing why you're doing them or where they came from."[17] Christian parents face the frustration of watching a program with their children only to scramble wildly in the attempt to shield them from a screen flashed to depravity.

---

[15] *All That Glitters*, 188.
[16] *Four Arguments*, 210.
[17] Ibid., 211.

We must take this attack on truth seriously and teach our children the biblical response to temptation—flight. While we ought not subject ourselves willingly to spiritually threatening situations, we have the opportunity to respond righteously when they arise.

A weaving together of four criteria—domination, industry, priority, and purposefulness—demonstrates the peril of entertainment once again. Television dominates the lives of many people. The statistics vary, but all tests on the subject present the dominating, even narcotic effect of television. Some surveys estimate that the average American child watches 25 hours of television per week.[18] Some estimates range even higher.[19] The United States Department of Labor attests that television absorbs more time that any other leisure activity.[20] In the process, for the average American it eats up over 18 hours per person per week that cannot be spent in purposeful, constructive activity. This amounts to over 10% of the 168 total hours available to a person in a week. While God plans for people to enjoy some entertainment or some time of rest and leisure, He does not desire slavish devotion to it. Modern culture worships entertainment. All sense of right priority and proportion in life bows to amusement. When we use television within the boundaries established by Scripture, we do not warrant criticism; but when television gains control and breeds sloth, misplaced priorities, and empty living, it becomes sinful for us regardless of its content.

As scathing as a denunciation of these propensities of television to violate biblical criteria may be, we still cannot legislate the right course of action by the imposition of a human standard. God does

---

[18]http://www.mediafamily.org/research/report_mqexecsum.shtml. The effect is not limited to America. Canadians exceed 13 hours per person. www.cbc.ca/canada/story/2004/10/17/Sleepsurvey_041017.html.

[19]See Barbour, 13, for an estimate of 30 hours per person average in America.

[20]It is the "leisure activity that occupied the most time (2.6 hours per day)" for average American adults. http://www.bls.gov/news.release/atus.nr0.htm.

that through His Word. A recognition of the tendency toward abuse in a form of entertainment prepares us to respond quickly and decisively where that abuse occurs.

A few weeks ago, I was walking around the block with my family and a friend's family when we were attacked by a large dog. Only a concerted, aggressive response kept us from being bitten. I haven't stopped walking around the block, but I am more alert now. I have prepared and carry countermeasures to such an attack in the future. May I suggest that Scripture warrants a similar response to entertainment in our culture? The fact that Satan stalks us to destroy us should make us vigilant, not anxious (1 Pet. 5:8). Such passages do not commission us to stop walking outside but to stop walking carelessly.

Television's weaknesses do not prohibit its use any more than the abuses of other forms of entertainment forbid their use. As believers, we should expect fallen humanity to distort every form of legitimate entertainment. The fact that some forms of music degrade the soul does not ban all music any more than the fact that some books' use of words for illicit purposes bans the use of words for righteous purposes. Consequently, to recognize a propensity for abuse of television should make us extremely and persistently wary of Satan's attacks through this venue without necessarily causing us to reject the medium altogether. As with all facets of life, we must test everything on the basis of Scripture before approving it (Phil. 1:10; 1 John 4:1).[21] We do not accept blindly anything that this world offers, nor do we reject blindly. We study this life for traps, for pitfalls, and for false roads, then turn away from all that leads us away from God.

---

[21]A person need not participate in sin in order to know that it is wrong. God's Word unequivocally defines some things to be evil. The Christian does not need to immerse himself in an activity in order to evaluate that activity objectively.

# CONCLUSION

Since he does not find specific statements on modern culture in Scripture, the believer must rely on a thoroughly biblical worldview coupled with biblically informed discernment to answer questions of life. Both are indispensable. Some Christians approach the entertainment of their age without a biblical worldview and end up floundering in the quagmire of personal choice. Others approach entertainment with a partially constructed biblical worldview but fail to discern legitimate applications in their age. We cannot excuse ourselves from either task. The Bible provides a comprehensive worldview that is truthful. It also establishes criteria by which each of us can evaluate the truthfulness of rival worldviews. People will continue to offer competing perspectives on humanity, the world, and ethics; but God has already established a guide that is both sufficient for and proficient in answering the questions that we face in our generation. The question of our entertainment is no different.

This work has presented a basic pattern of entertainment analysis.

First, we must have a biblical perspective on humanity and God-given pleasure.

Second, we must admit the scriptural grounds that disqualify entertainment—a direct violation of God's command or a personal misuse of pleasure in an excessive or harmful fashion.

Third, we must apply biblical criteria to determine whether our entertainment choices violate either of these scriptural grounds.

Fourth, we must examine our choices regularly to determine whether we are still using entertainment correctly or abusing it.

When we stand in a position anchored by the Scriptures and settled in a discerning conscience as upright, we then live rightly before the Lord. The wisest of men concludes his exploration of humanity with a clear biblical injunction: "Fear God and keep His commandments, for this is the whole duty of man. For God shall bring every work into judgment" (Eccles. 12:13–14). May each of us, as obedient children, heed this call.